1001 GROSSEST JOKES

IN THE WORLD...

...POSSIBLY THE UNIVERSE!

igloo

igloo

Published in 2012
by Igloo Books Ltd
Cottage Farm
Sywell
NN6 0BJ
www.igloo-books.com

C005 0312

2 4 6 8 10 9 7 5 3 1

ISBN: 978-0-85780-479-2

Printed and manufactured in China

Contents

Stinky

What do you call a smelly time traveller?

Doctor Poo!

What is the smelliest instrument in a brass band?

A trump-et!

What smells and sounds like a bell?

Dung!

All the toilets have been stolen from the police station...

... they have nothing to go on!

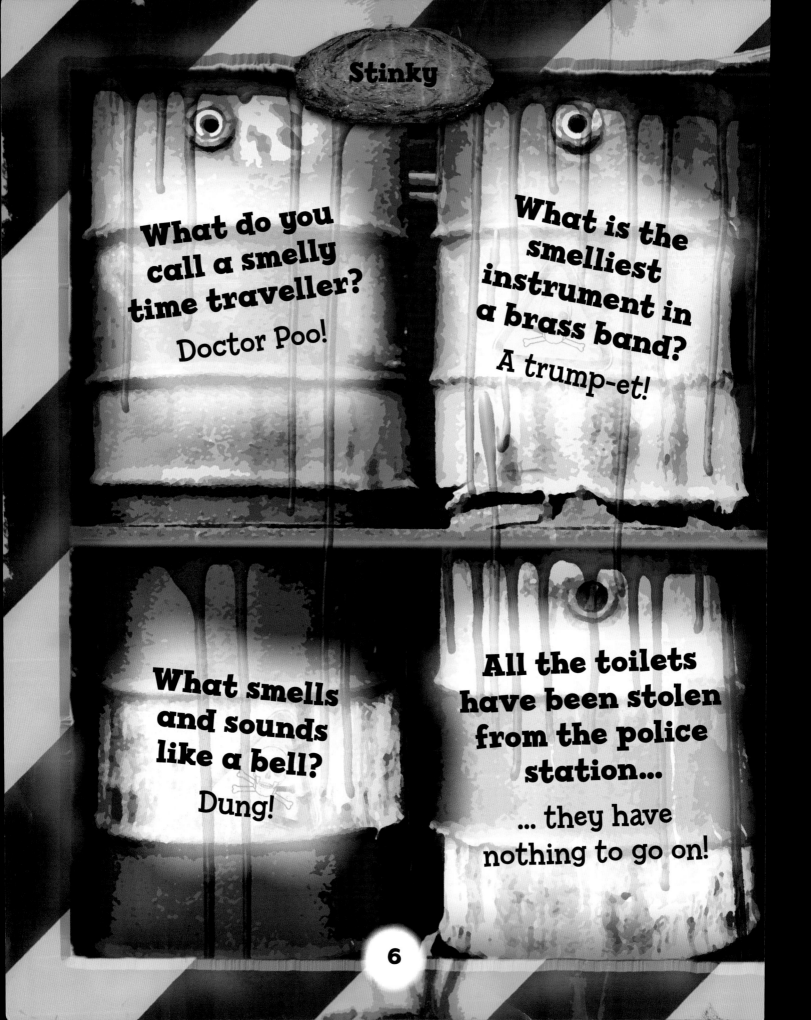

What do you call a flying skunk?

A smelli-copter!

What do you call a fairy who doesn't take a bath?

Stinker-bell!

Did you hear the joke about the fart?

It stinks!

Thomas: "Mum, please can I lick the bowl?"

Mum: "No! Flush it like everyone else!"

Why did Jason take his own toilet roll to the birthday party?

Because he was a party pooper!

What did the mouth say to the eye?

"Something between us smells!"

What are two robbers called?

A pair of nickers!

Why did Tigger have his head down the toilet?

Because he was looking for Pooh!

What did one toilet say to the other one?

"You look flushed!"

What did the boy fly say to the girl fly?

"Is this stool taken?"

Richard was walking down the street when he slipped on a pile of sick. He got up and started to walk away. He heard a yelp, behind him. Phillippa had slipped on the pile of stinky sick, too. He turned around, laughed and said, "I've just done that!" Phillippa was not impressed, "Well you could have cleaned it up!" she said.

What's brown and sticky?

A brown stick!

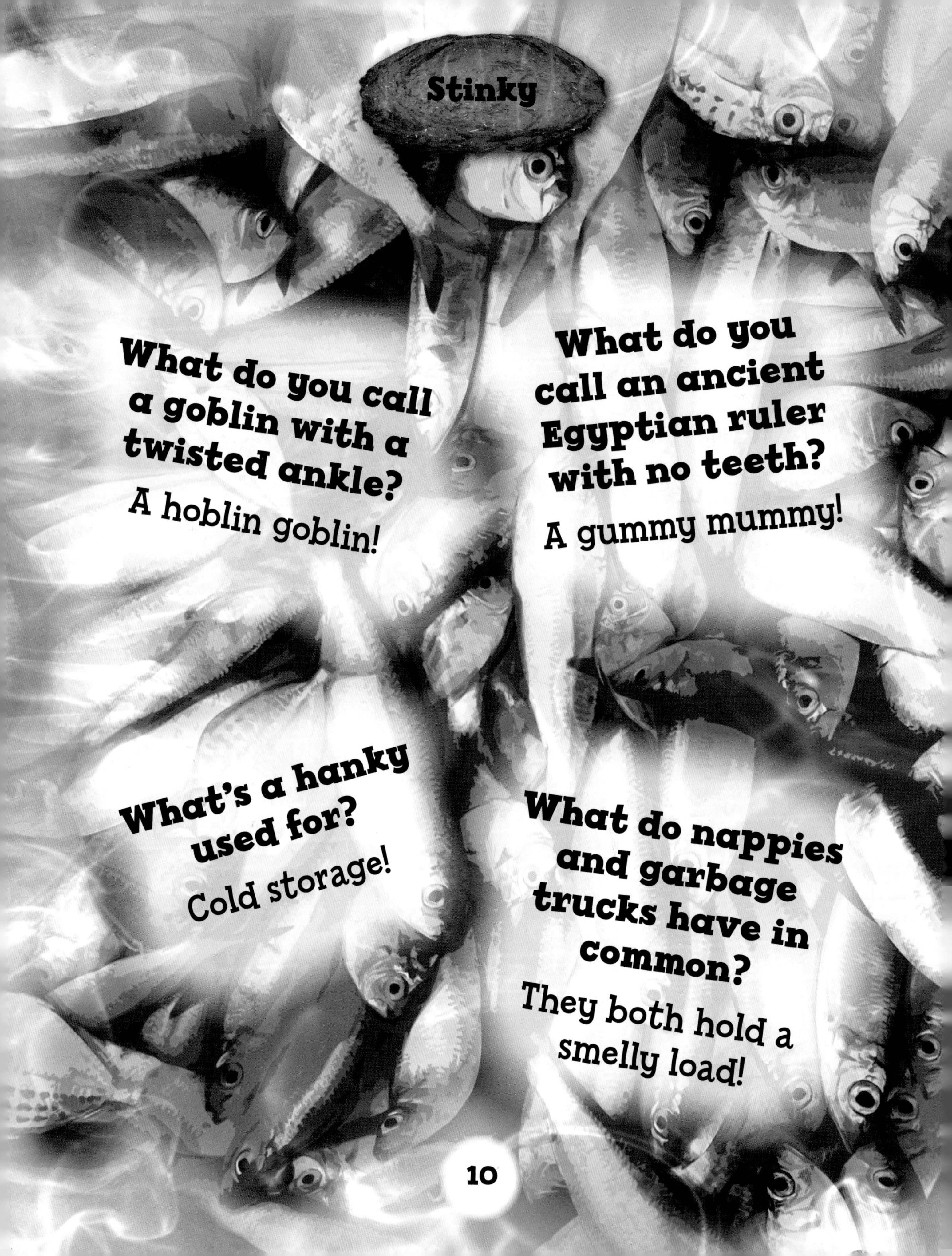

What do you call a goblin with a twisted ankle?

A hoblin goblin!

What do you call an ancient Egyptian ruler with no teeth?

A gummy mummy!

What's a hanky used for?

Cold storage!

What do nappies and garbage trucks have in common?

They both hold a smelly load!

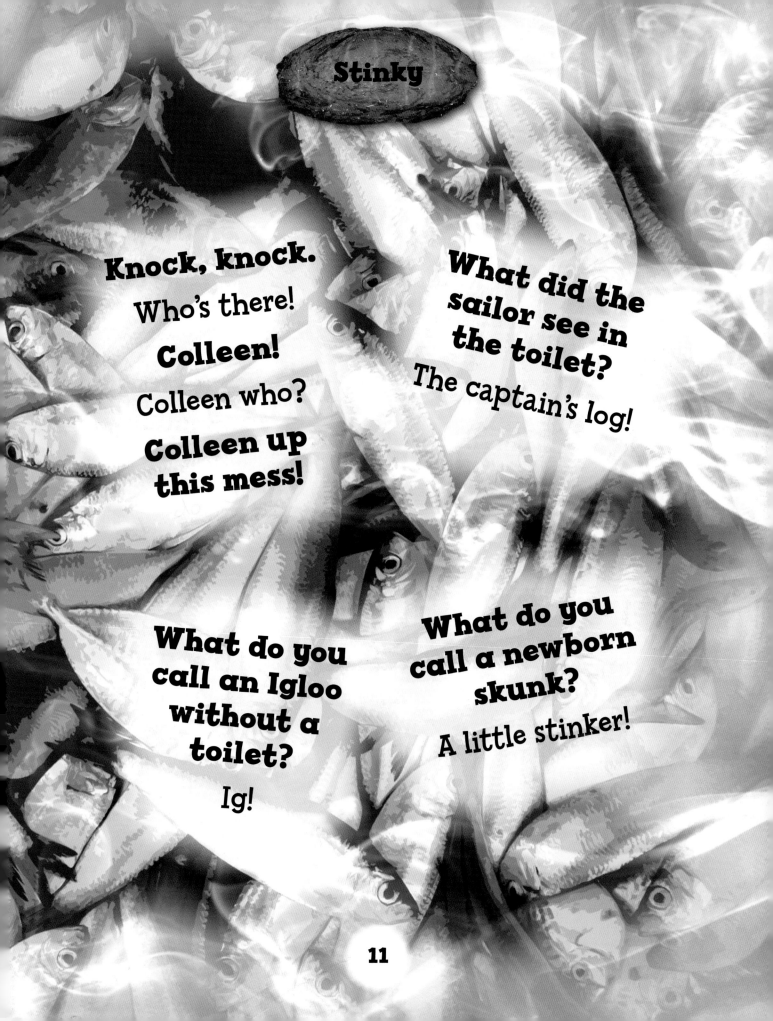

Stinky

Knock, knock.

Who's there!

Colleen!

Colleen who?

Colleen up this mess!

What did the sailor see in the toilet?

The captain's log!

What do you call an Igloo without a toilet?

Ig!

What do you call a newborn skunk?

A little stinker!

Stinky

What do you call a man who forgets to put his pants on?

Nicholas!

What flower is tall and smells?

A giraf-odill!

Knock, knock.

Who's there?

Smell mop.

Smell mop who?

Erm, no thanks!

How do you make a toilet roll?

Throw it down a hill!

Stinky

Boys are so dirty, the only time they wash their ears is when they eat a watermelon!

What happened when the dinosaur ate some brussel sprouts?

It did a jurassic fart!

Why does Tigger smell so bad?

Because he plays with Pooh all day!

What happens when you play table tennis with a bad egg?

First it goes ping, then it goes pong!

What do you call a huge, hairy, stinky beast?

King Pong!

What did the shoe say to the foot?

"This job really stinks!"

What did the submarine say to the ship?

"I can see your bottom!"

What tree can't you climb?

A lavatory!

What do you call an elephant that never washes?

A smelly-phant!

What do you get if you cross a Scottish monster with a bad egg?

The Loch Ness Pongster!

What do you call a woman with a toilet on her head?

Lou!

What do you get if you cross a worm with a toad?

A boy!

What do you get if you cross a skunk with a bear?

Winnie the Pooh!

What famous artist had one toilet upstairs and one downstairs?

Two-loos Lautrec!

What's green and smelly?

The Hulk farting!

How does a skunk call home?

On his smell-phone!

What do you call a woman with two toilets on her head?

Lulu!

My brother is built upside down...

... his nose runs and his feet smell!

What do you get if you cross martial arts with a deadly fart?

Kung Poo!

What's the smelliest city in America?

Poo York!

Why did the snooker player use the toilet?

He needed to pot the brown!

Why do traffic lights go red?

Well you would go red if you had to stop and go in the middle of the road!

Did you hear about the boy who put on a clean pair of socks every day?

By the end of the week he couldn't get his shoes on!

Why did the toilet roll down the hill?

To get to the bottom!

What gets wet as it dries?

A towel!

What's it called when you ignore a bad toilet?

Evil-loo-shun!

Stinky

Knock, knock.

Who's there?

Worzel.

Worzel who?

It's upstairs, first on the left!

What do flies and stinky feet have in common?

You can shoe them, but they never go away!

What's the smelliest hair style?

Pigtails!

Knock, knock.

Who's there?

Luke.

Luke who?

Luke out, here comes a big fart!

What do you get if you cross a boomerang with a skunk?

A stink you can't get rid of!

How do poos greet one another?

How do you do-do?

How do you define agony?

A one-armed man hanging from a cliff with an itchy bum!

What's the difference between a toilet brush and a biscuit?

Dunk them in your tea and you'll soon find out!

What did one toilet roll say to the other?

"People keep ripping me off!"

When is underwear like flowers in the garden?

When it's a pair of pink bloomers!

Why do boys have spots?

So they can play dot-to-dot!

What do you get if you cross a birthday cake and brussel sprouts?

A cake that blows out its own candles!

How do monsters begin fairy tales?

Once upon a slime!

What's the difference between a musician and a corpse?

One composes and the other decomposes!

What's long, rotten and smells of cheese?

Your toenails!

Knock, knock.

Who's there?

Danielle.

Danielle who?

Danielle at me, it was the dog!

What's the difference between a skunk and a boy?

Not much!

Knock, knock.

Who's there?

Jam!

Jam who?

Jam mind, I'd like some privacy in here!

What has a broom and flies?

A janitor covered in poo!

Did you ever see the movie 'Constipated'?

It never came out!

Knock, knock.

Who's there?

Hallie.

Hallie who?

Hallie-tosis, your breath stinks!

What do you get if you cross a skunk with a dinosaur?

A stinka-saurus!

What do stinky boys wear?

Dung-garees!

Why did the man put his eye in the freezer?

He wanted to make an eye-cicle!

What happened to the thief who stole a ton of prunes?

He was on the run for weeks!

Stinky

Knock, knock.

Who's there?

Armageddon.

Armageddon who?

Armageddon out of here, it stinks!

What's frozen water?

Ice.

What's frozen cream?

Ice-cream.

What's frozen tea?

Iced tea.

What's frozen ink?

Iced ink.

Phew, you do – go take a shower!

Who is green and eats porridge?

Mouldy Locks!

Why did the man eat ten tins of baked beans?

He wanted to go windsurfing!

Knock, knock.

Who's there?

Nicholas.

Nicholas who?

Nicholas girls shouldn't climb trees!

They say ignorance is bliss. That's why boys are always so happy!

What books do skunks like to read?

Best-smellers!

Knock, knock.

Who's there?

Sarah.

Sarah who?

Sarah bad smell in the room?

Stinky

What did the judge say when the silent but deadly fart was on trial?

"Odour in court!"

How do you cope with a gas leak?

Send the person out of the room and open the window!

Why did the fish smell so bad?

Long time, no sea!

Do you want to hear some more fart jokes?

No, they really stink!

space

School

What instrument did the skeleton play in the school orchestra?

A trom-bone!

What happened to the naughty little witch at school?

She was ex-spelled!

What language does a billboard speak?

Sign language!

What's the difference between school dinners and a pile of worms?

School dinners are on plates!

Teacher: "What would you do if I came to school with a face as dirty as yours?"

Pupil: "Nothing, Miss, I'm far too polite!"

What did the ghost teacher say to his class?

Don't spook until you're spooken to!

What's the most important thing to remember in chemistry?

Never, ever, lick the spoon!

Teacher: "Here's a percentage question: If there are ten questions and you get ten correct, what do you get?"

Pupil: "Accused of cheating!"

What's tall, orange, wears glasses and carries a pile of books?

A carrot disguised as a teacher!

Teacher: "If you breathe oxygen during the day, what do you breathe at night?"

Pupil: "Nitrogen!"

Why did the class joker go to hospital?

To learn some sick jokes!

In school assembly the piano teacher's performance was cheered and cheered.

The piano was locked up!

Teacher: "Have you thought about what you're giving your Mum for Christmas?"

Pupil: "Yes, a list of what I want!"

Where do ghosts study?

Ghoul-lege!

Teacher: "Why have you got a sausage behind your ear?"

Pupil: "Oh, no! I must have eaten my pencil for lunch!"

Why was the cannibal so popular at school?

He kept buttering up the teachers!

Teacher: "You missed school yesterday didn't you?"

Pupil: "Not very much!"

What happened to the carpentry teacher's car?

Wooden start!

Why are there whales at the bottom of the ocean?

Because they dropped out of school!

What after-school club do vampire children join?

A blood group!

What's the difference between teachers and chocolate?

Children like chocolate!

What's black and white and hard all over?

An exam paper!

What meals do math teachers like most?

Take aways!

Teacher: "Are you homesick?"

Pupil: "No, I'm here sick!"

Why are peacocks so unpopular in school?

They're always spreading tales!

What has a spine, but no bones?

A book!

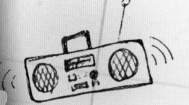

Teacher: "What happened when electricity was discovered?"

Pupil: "Someone got a nasty shock!"

What do young ghosts write their homework in?

An exorcise book!

Teacher: "You look pale today."

Pupil: "I think I over-washed!"

Teacher: "What's the difference between ignorance and apathy?"

Pupil: "I don't know and I don't care!"

Why did the flea fail his exams?

He wasn't up to scratch!

Teacher: "Are you good at arithmetic?"

Pupil: "Yes and no."

Teacher: "What do you mean?"

Pupil: "Yes, I am no good at arithmetic!"

Tom: "Our history teacher has long black hair all the way down her back."

Josh: "It's a pity it doesn't grow on her head!"

What's green and dangerous and good at arithmetic?

A crocodile with a calculator!

Why were the school books so depressed?

They were full of problems!

What did the skunk enjoy most about school?

Show and smell!

Pupil: "Miss, can I have another glass of water?"

Cookery teacher: "But that's your tenth glass, what are you making that needs 10 glasses of water?"

Pupil: "Nothing, it's just that the notice board is still on fire!"

What's the yuckiest, stickiest, gunkiest instrument in the school orchestra?

The flu-te!

Why was Matt locked in a cage in the corner of the classroom?

He was the teacher's pet!

Where's the best place for the school sickroom?

Next to the dining hall!

What's stringy, green, wears glasses and carries a pile of books?

A bogey disguised as a teacher!

When I was at school I was as bright as the next boy...

... it's just a shame the next boy was such an idiot!

Teacher: "Why are you standing on your head?"

Pupil: "You told us to turn things over in our heads!"

What's the first thing vampires learn at school?

The alpha-bat!

Why did the nose not want to go to school?

He was always getting picked on!

Knock, knock.

Who's there?

Ida.

Ida who?

Ida awful time at school today!

Teacher: "This is the third time I've had to tell you off this week, what have you got to say about that?"
Pupil: "Thank goodness it's Friday!"

What's a mushroom?

The school dining hall!

What do you call a person who talks when nobody is listening?

A teacher!

What kind of cake do you get after school dinners?

Stomach-cake!

Cross-eyed Monster: "When I grow up I want to be a bus driver."

Careers Advisor: "Well I won't stand in your way!"

Teacher: "Name three collective nouns."

Pupil: "Wastepaper bin, garbage truck and vacuum cleaner!"

Teacher: "Why didn't you look up rhinos on your laptop?"

Pupil: "I didn't want a squashed lap, sir!"

Sarah: "How come you did so badly in the history test? You had all the answers written on your sleeve."

Hannah: "I had my geography shirt on by mistake!"

What's big, smelly, wears glasses and carries a pile of books?

A teacher!

What's the difference between a school teacher and a train?

One says, "Spit that gum out!" and the other says, "Choo, choo!"

Why did the one-eyed monster give up teaching?

He only had one pupil!

Teacher: "How many books have you read in your lifetime?"

Pupil: "I don't know, I'm not dead yet!"

What's the most popular sentence at school?

I don't know!

Teacher: "Why do you always get so dirty?"

Pupil: "Because I'm a lot closer to the ground than you are!"

Teacher: "Why shouldn't you mention the number 288 in polite company?"

Pupil: "Because it's two gross!"

Did you hear about the cross-eyed teacher?

He couldn't control his pupils!

What do you get if you cross the school bell with an alarm clock?

Something that wakes you up when it's time to go home!

How do you keep flies out of the school dining hall?

Let them taste the food!

Teacher: "Your work is inconsistent. Your last essay was great, but this one I can't read."

Pupil: "My Mum is a better writer than my Dad!"

Teacher: "If I lay one egg here and another two over there, how many eggs will there be?"

Pupil: "None."

Teacher: "Why not?"

Pupil: "Because you can't lay eggs!"

Teacher: "What do you call an old volcano?"

Pupil: "A blast from the past!"

Why did the teacher put the lights on?

Because the class was so dim!

Which school did the cannibal go to?

Eat-on!

What did Shakespeare enjoy most about school?

Play time!

The class went on a school trip to the natural history museum.

Mum: "How was it?"

Tom: "Rubbish."

Mum: "Why?"

Tom: "It's the worst zoo I've ever been to, all the animals were dead!"

What's the worst thing you will find in a school dining hall?

The food!

Teacher: "If there were five crows in a tree and the farmer shot one, how many would be left?"

Pupil: "None, they'd have all flown away!"

What's the difference between homework and onions?

Nobody cries when you chop up homework!

Teacher: "Why are you late again?"

Pupil: "There was a sign outside, it said, 'school ahead, go slow'!"

Scary

Who is the best dancer at the monster's ball?

The Boogie Man!

Why was the ghost hunter so fit?

He exorcised regularly!

What did the daddy cannibal say to his son at tea time?

"Don't talk with someone in your mouth!"

What do witches play at parties?

Hide-and-Shriek!

Why aren't ghosts any good at lying?

You can see right through them!

What pet does Dracula have?

A Blood Hound!

What do you call a monster that eats his mother and father?

An orphan!

What happened when the Abominable Snowman had chilli for dinner?

He melted!

What game do monsters love to play at parties?

Swallow the leader!

Why don't skeletons like roller coasters?

They don't have the guts!

Why did the zombie stay in his coffin all day?

He felt rotten!

How does a monster greet you?

Pleased to eat you!

What do you say to a three-headed monster?

"Hello, hello, hello!"

How can you help a hungry cannibal?

Give him a helping hand!

What do ghosts like on their chops?

Grave-y!

How do you make a witch itch?

Take away the W!

What does a skeleton order at a restaurant?

Spare ribs!

Why is Dracula so thin?

He eats necks to nothing!

What do sea monsters snack on between meals?

Potato ships!

Which ghost ate the three bears' porridge?

Ghoul-dilocks!

Why are zombies always tired?

Because they are dead on their feet!

What do you call a monster with a high IQ?

Frank-Einstein!

What do you call a monster who eats his father's sister?

An aunt-eater!

What music do zombies shake their stuff to?

Soul music!

What do witches use for racing each other?

Vrooom-sticks!

What fruit does Dracula like best?

Neck-tarines!

What do Italian ghosts eat?

Spook-ghetti!

Why don't cannibals eat weather forecasters?

They give them wind!

Why did the Cyclops give up teaching?

He only had one pupil!

What do sea monsters like to eat?

Fish and ships!

Why did the skeleton have no get up and go?

He was a lazy bones!

What did the father ghost say to his son?

"Spook when you're spooken to!"

What do you call a witch without a broomstick?

A witch-hiker!

What do you get when King Kong steps on Batman and Robin?

Flatman and Ribbon!

What do you get if you cross a werewolf with a cow?

A burger that bites back!

Who is the world-famous skeleton detective?

Sherlock Bones!

What does Dr. Jekyll play with his friends?

Hyde-and-seek!

What do ghosts with a sweet tooth enjoy?

Boo-ble gum!

What ride do ghosts like at the fair?

The roller-ghoster!

Two monsters are eating a clown...

... one says to the other, "Does this taste funny to you?"

What hairstyle did the hippy monster have?

Deadlocks!

What do you call a ghost's mum and dad?

Trans-parents!

What happens when a vampire drinks too much blood?

He gets a fang-over!

How do witches keep their elaborate hairstyles in place?

Scare-spray!

What function does a witch find useful on a computer?

The spell-checker!

Who works in monster offices?

A skeleton staff!

Why didn't the skeleton go to the party?

He had nobody to go with!

What did the short-sighted monster wear?

Spook-tacles!

Why did the angry witch fall off her broom?

She flew off the handle!

What do posh skeletons use at dinner parties?

Bone china!

What is the correct way to greet a ghost?

"How do you boo?"

What music do mummies like to dance to?

Ragtime!

Why are zombies never lonely?

They can always dig up a few old friends!

Why are cemeteries so popular?

Who knows, but people are dying to get into them!

What boats do vampires sail in?

Blood vessels!

What kind of cheese do monsters like?

Monster-ella!

Why was the Egyptian mummy such a loner?

He was too wrapped up in himself!

Where do ghosts go on holiday?

Death Valley!

Why does Dracula enjoy ballroom dancing so much?

He loves the vaultz!

How can you tell if a zombie has a cold?

He starts coffin!

Why was the skeleton laughing?

Someone had tickled his funny bone!

What do you call a floating sea monster?

Bob!

What do you call two witches that share a room?

Broom-mates!

What did the barman say when the ghost ordered a gin and tonic?

"Sorry, we don't serve spirits!"

Why did the skeleton refuse dinner?

He didn't have the stomach for it!

What did one cool ghost say to the other?

"Get a life!"

What do you call a monster who hangs from the walls?

Art!

What do ghosts watch at the theatre?

Phanto-mimes!

Why is it bad news when you upset a cannibal?

You end up in hot water!

What airlines do monsters use?

British Scareways!

What do you do when you see a monster sitting in your car?

Walk!

What kind of ghosts haunt hospitals?

Surgical spirits!

What do you call a witch in the distance?

Dot!

What do you get when you cross a witch with Jack Frost?

A cold spell!

Why are vampires so artistic?

They are great at drawing blood!

What do witches sit on?

Toadstools!

Where do zombies go on holiday?

The Dead Sea!

Which dance do vampires excel in?

Fang-dango!

What do you call a skeleton rock band?

The Strolling Bones!

What is the first part of a newspaper that a monster turns to?

The horror-scope!

What do you get if you cross a snowman with a vampire?

Frostbite!

What did the monster say when he was full?

"I couldn't eat another mortal!"

What do get when you cross a vampire with a plumber?

A bloodbath!

Did you hear about the new Dracula film?

It's fang-tastic!

What do you call a monster covered in leaves?

Russell!

What do vampires do at 11am?

They take a coffin break!

What is a vampire's snack of choice?

A fang-furter!

How does a witch tell the time?

With her witch watch!

What do get if you cross a monster with a Boy Scout?

A creature that scares old ladies across the road!

What is a devil's picket line called?

A demon-stration!

What happened when Ray met a monster?

He became an ex-Ray!

Why is the graveyard so noisy?

Because of all the coffin!

What do you call a monster with gravy, meat and potatoes on his head?

Stew!

Where does Dracula keep his savings?

In the blood bank!

Why were the workers frightened of their dragon boss?

He kept firing people!

When do zombies cook their victims?

On Fry-day!

What do you do with a blue monster?

Try and cheer him up!

Who writes invisible books?

A ghost writer!

Can you name the famous witch detective?

Warlock Holmes!

What's green and hides away in bedrooms at parties?

The Incredible Sulk!

Where did the skeleton buy his girlfriend's birthday present?

The body shop!

Why is the letter V like a monster?

It comes after U!

What monster makes funny noises in its throat?

A gargoyle!

What is the best way to speak to a monster?

From a long distance!

What happened to the monster who ran away with the circus?

His mummy made him take it back!

What kind of horse would a headless horseman ride?

A knight-mare!

What do you call a yeti in a phone box?

Stuck!

Where do British witches go on holiday?

To the Isle of Fright!

Why does Dracula have no friends?

Because he's a pain in the neck!

What noise does a witch's breakfast make?

Snap, cackle and pop!

What do you call zombies in a belfry?

Dead ringers!

How do you stop a monster from smelling?

Cut off his nose!

Why did the two Cyclops flight?

They could never see eye to eye over anything!

What do you call a monster who likes sewing?

Fred!

What do you call a huge, ugly, slobbering, furry monster with cotton wool in his ears?

Anything you like, he can't hear you!

Where do ghosts pick up their mail?

At the ghost office!

What coffee does Dracula like best?

De-coffiin-ated!

What kind of monster has the best hearing?

The eeriest!

Monster: "Where do fleas go in winter?"

Werewolf: "Search me!"

If you want to know more about Dracula, what do you have to do?

Join his fang club!

What do you get if you cross a dinosaur with a wizard?

A Tyrannosaurus hex!

What kind of roads do ghosts haunt?

Dead Ends!

Who won the skeleton beauty contest?

No body!

Where do baby ghosts go during the day?

Day-scare centres!

What does a witch ask for when she goes to a hotel?

Broom-service!

Did you hear about the skeleton that was ambushed by a dog?

The dog ran off with two bones and the skeleton was left without a leg to stand on!

What is evil, ugly, dressed in black and goes round and round?

A witch in a revolving door!

What do you get if you cross a vampire with Al Capone?

A fang-ster!

What do you call a vampire that's always feeling peckish?

Snack-ula!

What kind of tie does a monster wear to a formal party?

A boo-tie!

What do you call a wicked old woman who lives by the sea?

A sand-witch!

What is evil and ugly on the inside and green on the outside?

A witch dressed as a cucumber!

What do you get if you cross a monster with a pig?

Large pork chops!

What is ugly, scary and purple?

A monster holding its breath!

What happened when the werewolf swallowed a clock?

It got ticks!

Why couldn't the swamp monster go to the party?

Because he was bogged down in his work!

What has a green spotted body, ten hairy legs and big eyes on stalks?

I don't know, but there is one crawling up your leg!

What is the American national day for vampires?

Fangs-giving Day!

What do monsters send home while on holiday?

Ghost-cards!

History

What was Camelot?

A place where people parked their camels!

How did the Vikings send secret messages?

By norse code!

What did the executioner say to the prisoner?

"Time to head off!"

Why were the early days of history called the dark ages?

Because there were so many knights!

Which king had the noisiest bottom?

King Richard the Lion-fart!

Who made King Arthur's round table?

Sir-Cumference!

Why did Henry VIII have so many wives?

He liked to chop and change!

Why is the ghost of Anne Boleyn always running after the ghost of Henry VIII?

She's trying to get ahead!

Why did Robin Hood only rob the rich?

Because the poor didn't have anything worth stealing!

What's vicious, Victorian and lives at the bottom of the sea?

Jack the Kipper!

Where did knights learn to kill dragons?

At knight school!

What do you call a Roman emperor with the flu?

Julius Sneezer!

Did you hear about the Roman slave who had his ears chopped off as punishment?

He was never heard of again!

Did you hear about the tense mummy?

He was really wound up!

What do you call a pirate with four eyes?

A piiiirate!

Why was the Egyptian prince so upset?

He woke up to find his Daddy was now a Mummy!

Why did the one-handed pirate cross the road?

He wanted to get to the second-hand shop!

Where does Napoleon keep his armies?

Up his sleevies!

How was the Roman Empire cut in half?

With a pair of rusty Caesars!

Why did the knight pull out of the archery contest?

He found it an arrowing experience!

What did the dragon say when he saw the knight in shining armor?

"I hate tinned food!"

What did Caesar say after Brutus stabbed him?

"Ow!"

Why do mummies not tell secrets?

They keep everything under wraps!

Did you hear about the time Henry VIII farted in court?

It caused a royal stink!

What was the fruit that launched a thousand ships?

Melon of Troy!

Which queen burped a lot?

Queen Hictoria!

Why was King Arthur's army too tired to fight?

Too many sleepless knights!

What do you put on the gravestone of a knight in shining armor?

Rust in peace!

What happened when Queen Victoria farted?

She issued a royal pardon!

Why did the executioner start work early?

He wanted to get a-head!

Where were traitors beheaded?

Just above their shoulders!

Why did Anne Boleyn not stand still when she was being executed?

She fancied a run around the block!

What's a gelatine?

An ancient device for chopping the heads off jelly babies!

What do kings do with their rotting teeth?

Get them crowned!

Who was England's smelliest king?

Richard the Turd!

What did the executioner say to the criminal in the guillotine?

"Heads, I win!"

Queen Victoria was on the throne from 1837 to 1901...

... that's a bad case of constipation!

When did Henry VIII die?

Just before they buried him!

Who was the most reasonable king of Egypt?

Pharaoh Nuff!

Why did Julius Ceasar buy permanent ink pens?

He wanted to 'Mark Anthony' forever!

Why did Cleopatra take milk baths?

She couldn't find a cow tall enough for a shower!

What's brown and sits on a piano stool?

Mozart's last movement!

Where do executioners work?

Head office!

Why is it always so yucky and wet in Britain?

The kings and queens keep reigning!

What do you call a mosquito in chain mail?

A bite in shining armor!

What kind of lighting did Noah use for the ark?

Flood lights!

What did William the Conqueror say when he fell down the loo?

"Weeeeeeeeeeeeeee!"

What happened when the gladiator put his head in the lion's mouth to count his teeth?

The lion closed his mouth to see how many heads the gladiator had!

What game did King Arthur like playing most?

Knights and crosses!

What's a guillotine?

A pain in the neck!

What's two hundred years old and lies at the bottom of the ocean, twitching?

A nervous wreck!

What did the prisoner say when he was put on the rack?

"Looks as if I'll be here for a l-o-n-g stretch!"

Which Egyptian queen liked to walk around in her underwear?

Cleo-pantra!

What do executioners write in December?

Their Christmas chopping lists!

During which age did the mummies live?

The band-age!

What do you call a highwayman with a cough and a dribble of snot running from his nose?

Sick Turpin!

What do Alexander the Great and Kermit the Frog have in common?

The same middle name!

What did dinosaurs have that no others animals ever had?

Baby dinosaurs!

What do pirates use soap for?

To wash themselves ashore!

What did the WWI cannon say to the WWII mine?

"You're a blast!"

Why would you use Cleopatra to draw a straight line?

She was an ancient ruler!

How much did the captain's treasure cost?

An arm and a leg!

What's purple and burns?

The Grape Fire of London!

Which historical figure was an expert on the springboard?

Lady Good-diver!

Why did it take Long John Silver so long to learn the alphabet?

He spent years at 'C'!

What was the middle ages famous for?

Its knight life!

What do you get in a five star pyramid?

A tomb with a view!

Who succeeded the first President of the United States?

The second one!

What would you get hanging from the walls of a Tudor castle?

Tired arms!

What is Queen Vic short for?

So she can tickle her toes!

What did the pirate say as he fell over board?

Water-way to go!

What do you call a Tyrannosaurus rex that talks and talks and talks?

A dino-bore!

What do hangmen read?
Noose-papers!

What is Beethoven doing in his grave?
De-composing!

Where did the Vikings land when they invaded Britain?
On their feet!

Why was the pirate cross when the toilet was out of order?
Because any pirate without a 'p' becomes irate!

Where do pirates go to let their hair down?

The beach ball!

Why are there old dinosaur bones in the museum?

Because they can't afford new ones!

Why is history like an old fruit cake?

It's full of dates!

What do you call a sleeping dinosaur?

A dino-snore!

What's the difference between a pirate and a bargain hunter?

One sails the sea, the other sees the sales!

What do you call a caveman who's been buried since the stone age?

Pete!

Why do dinosaurs eat raw meat?

Because they don't know how to cook!

How do you use an ancient Egyptian doorbell?

Toot-and-come-in!

When did the Vikings invade Britain?

During a plunder storm!

Why did King Arthur have a round table?

So no one could corner him!

Why do cavemen avoid dinosaurs?

Because their eggs stink!

Did you hear the dirty rumour about the empty pyramid?

There was nothing in it!

Creepy Crawlies

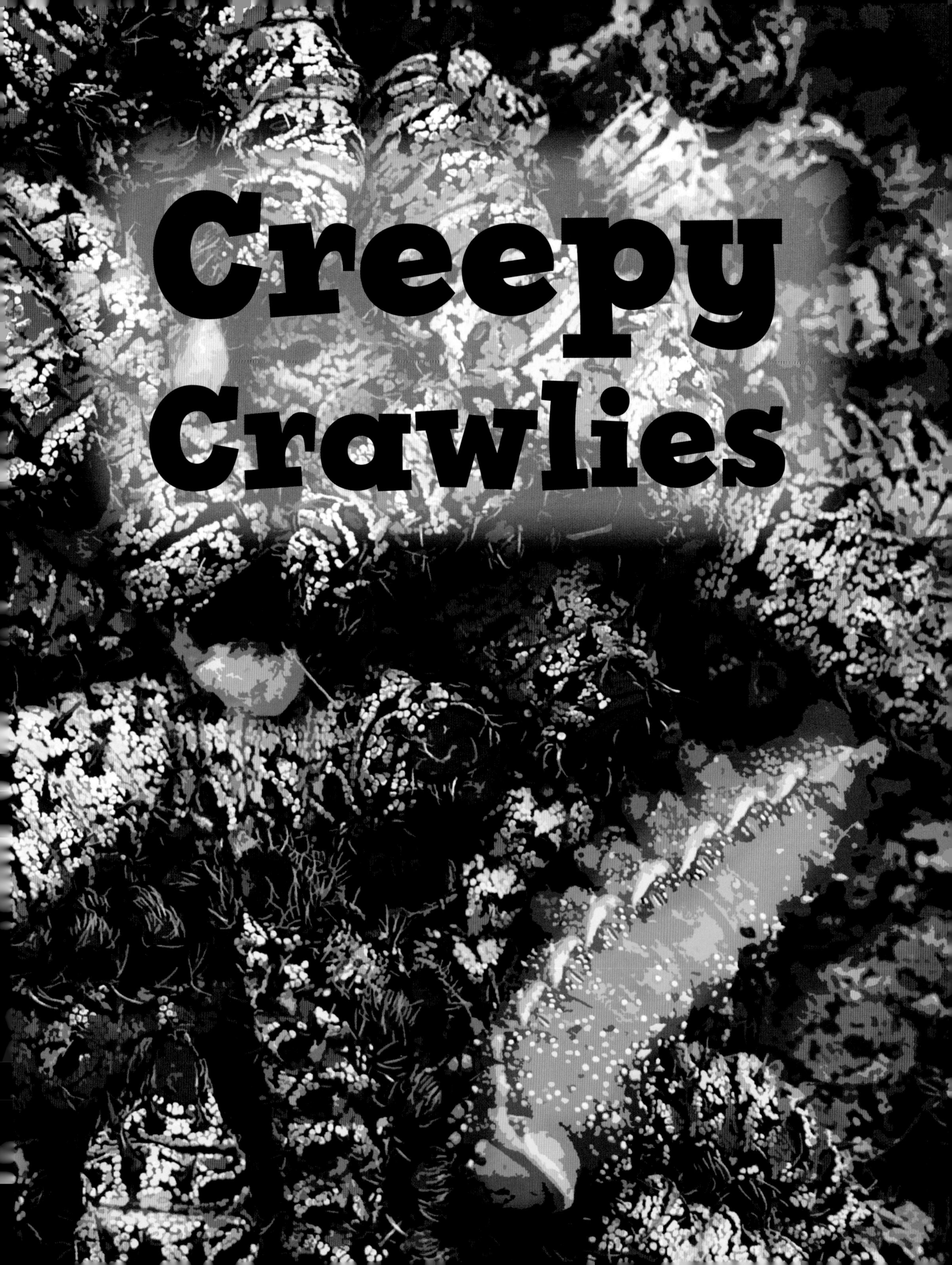

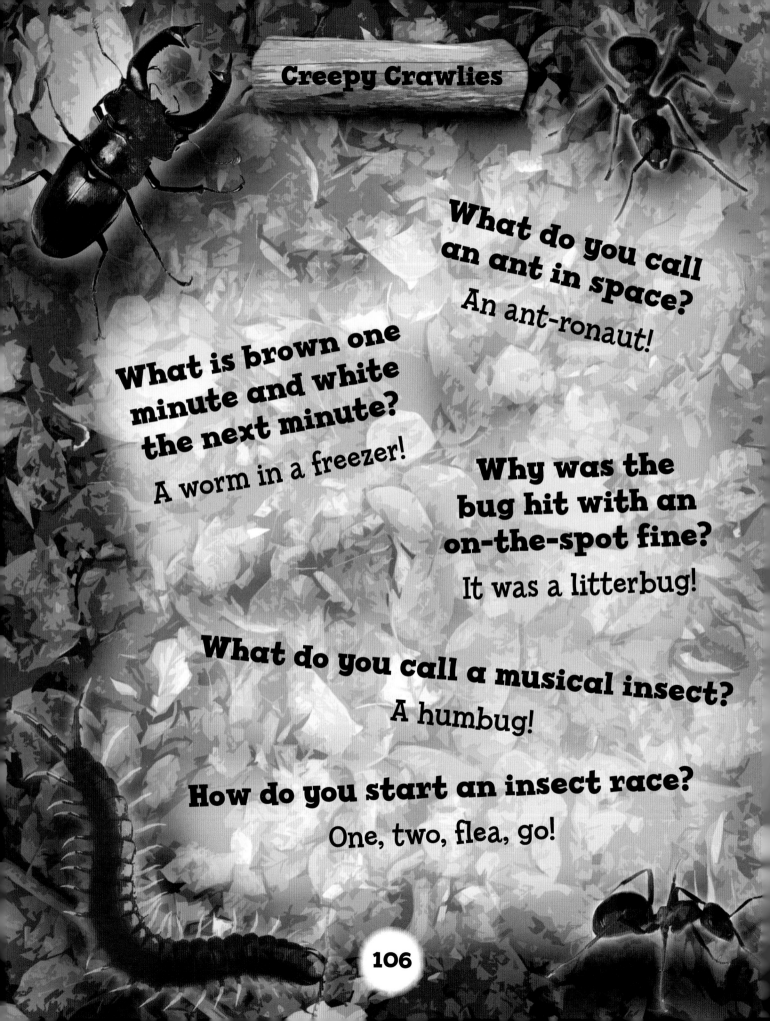

What do you call an ant in space?

An ant-ronaut!

What is brown one minute and white the next minute?

A worm in a freezer!

Why was the bug hit with an on-the-spot fine?

It was a litterbug!

What do you call a musical insect?

A humbug!

How do you start an insect race?

One, two, flea, go!

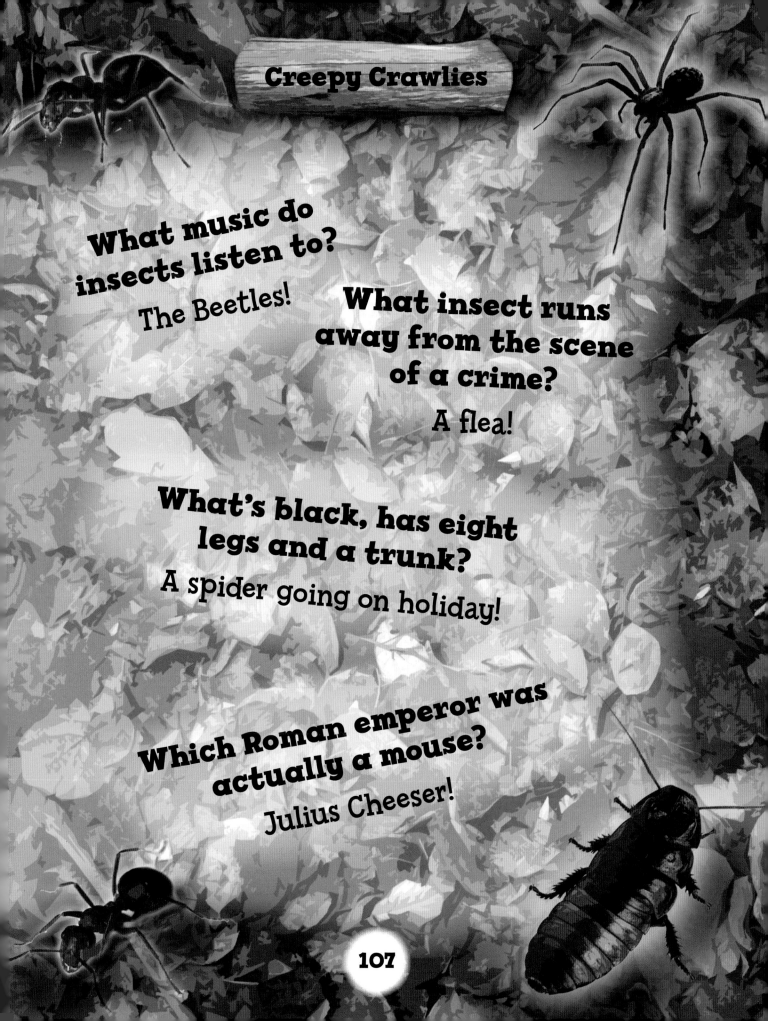

What music do insects listen to?

The Beetles!

What insect runs away from the scene of a crime?

A flea!

What's black, has eight legs and a trunk?

A spider going on holiday!

Which Roman emperor was actually a mouse?

Julius Cheeser!

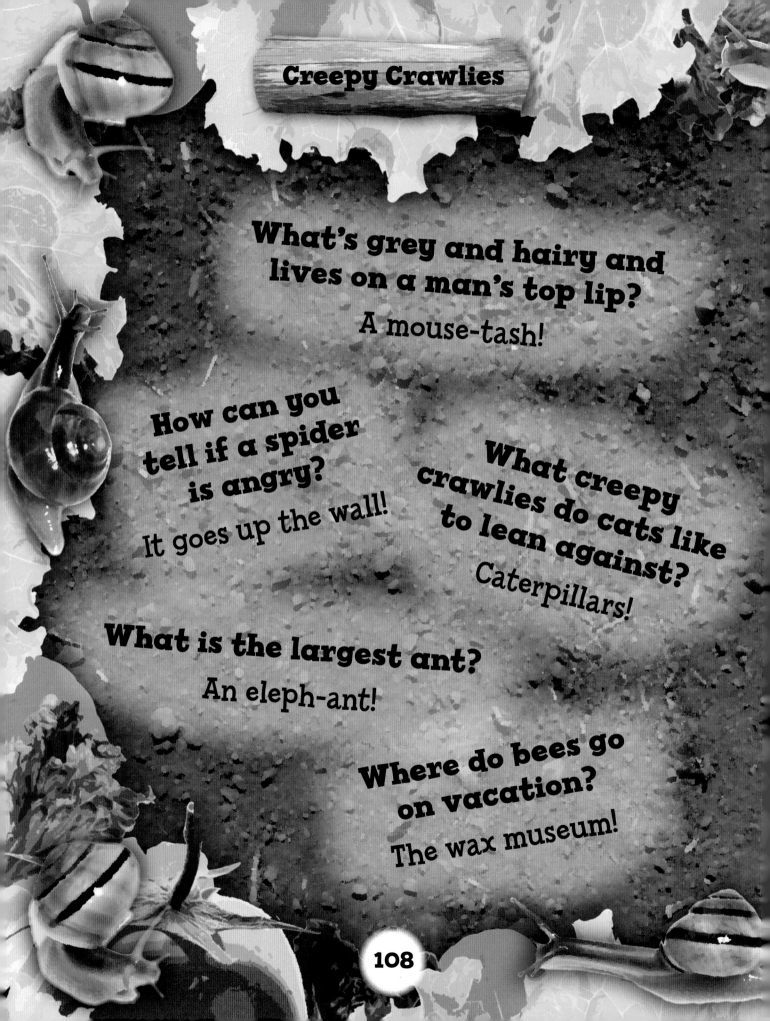

What's grey and hairy and lives on a man's top lip?

A mouse-tash!

How can you tell if a spider is angry?

It goes up the wall!

What creepy crawlies do cats like to lean against?

Caterpillars!

What is the largest ant?

An eleph-ant!

Where do bees go on vacation?

The wax museum!

What do you give a snake with a headache?

Asp-rin!

Why do bees buzz?

They find it difficult to whistle!

Who do wasps like to listen to?

Sting!

What bee is hard to hear?

A mumble bee!

What did the wasp say to the bee?

"Your honey or your life!"

What do you get if you cross ants with a rabbit?

Bugs Bunny!

Why were the little beetles grounded?

They were bugging their parents!

What was the worm doing in the corn field?

Going in one ear and out the other!

What do you call a bug that's worked its way to the top?

Head lice!

What do you call tired bugs?

Sleepy crawlies!

What do you call a fly with no wings?

A walk!

What do you call a fly with no wings or legs?

A raisin!

What do you get if you cross an electric eel with a sponge?

A shock absorber!

What's wriggly, dangerous and goes, "Hith, hith"?

A snake with a lisp!

Where do ill wasps go?

Wasp-ital!

Where do wasps and bees go for their holidays?

Sting-apore!

What did the bee say to the flower?

"Hello honey!"

Why are moths so unpopular?

They pick holes in everything!

What type of bee is good for your health?

Vitamin B-ee!

What do bees chew?

Bumble gum!

Why did the hedgehog cross the road?

To see his squash partner!

"Waiter, there are two flies in my soup!"

"Don't worry, Sir, we don't charge for the extra one!"

What do you call fishing when you don't catch any fish?

Drowning worms!

What lives in gum trees?

Stick insects!

Why did the lizard go on a diet?

It weighed too much for its scales!

Why did the blob always stay home?

He had no place to goo!

Why did the moth nibble a hole in the carpet?

He wanted to see the floor show!

What did the bus driver say to the Frog?

"Hop on!"

Why did the mosquito go to the dentist?

To improve his bite!

How many legs does an ant have?

The same as your uncle!

What did the slime say to the mould when they saw each other after a long time?

"You gruesome since I saw you last!"

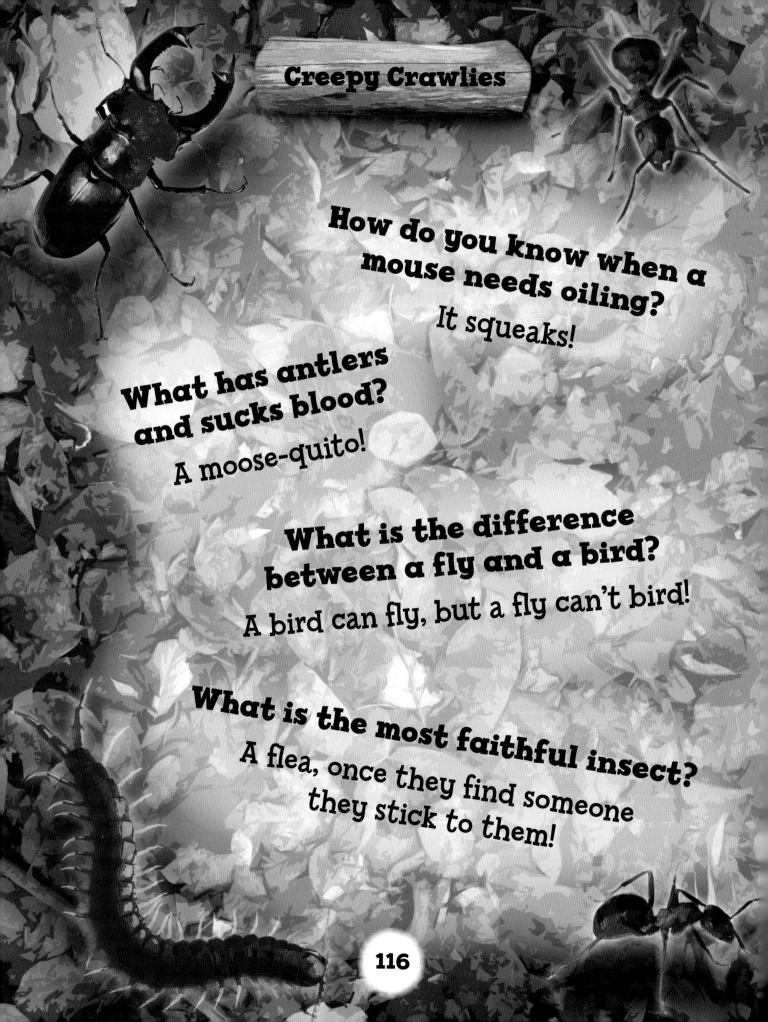

How do you know when a mouse needs oiling?

It squeaks!

What has antlers and sucks blood?

A moose-quito!

What is the difference between a fly and a bird?

A bird can fly, but a fly can't bird!

What is the most faithful insect?

A flea, once they find someone they stick to them!

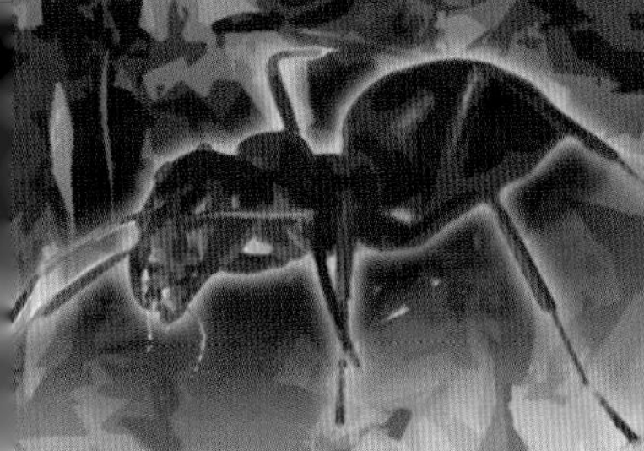

What game do elephants play with ants?

Squash!

What do you call two spiders who just got married?

Newly-webs!

What kind of bees fight?

Rumble bees!

What has six legs, bites and talks in code?

A morse-quito!

What did the fly say when he hit the car windscreen?

"That's me all over!"

Why was the insect thrown out of the forest?

Because he was a litter bug!

Patient: "Doctor, doctor, I keep thinking I'm a caterpillar."

Doctor: "Don't worry, you'll change soon!"

What's the difference between a worm and a cockroach?

Cockroaches crunch more when you eat them!

"Waiter, there's a dead beetle in my gravy."

"Yes, Sir. Beetles are terrible swimmers!"

What did the spider say to the beetle?

"Stop bugging me!"

Where do you find giant snails?

At the end of a giant's finger!

Patient: "Doctor, doctor, I keep seeing insects flying around my head."

Doctor: "It's just a bug that's going around!"

What do you get if you cross a baby and a spider?

A creepy crawler!

Which creepy crawlies are at the cutting edge of technology?

Spiders, they have their own websites!

What's the scariest insect?

A zom-bee!

What did the snake say when he was offered a piece of cheese for dinner?

"Thank you, I'll just have a slither!"

What did one slug say to another who had hit him and rushed off?

"I'll get you next slime!"

What did the slug say as he slipped down the window very fast?

"How slime flies!"

How do you know your kitchen is filthy?

The slugs leave trails on the floor that read, 'clean me'!

What do you get if you cross a glow-worm with a pint of beer?

Light ale!

What did the woodworm say to the chair?

"It's been nice gnawing you!"

What did one maggot say to another?

"What's a nice girl like you doing in a joint like this?"

What is the best advice to give a worm?

Sleep late!

What kind of wig can hear?

An earwig!

How do you keep flies out of the kitchen?

Put a pile of manure in the living room!

Why did the fly fly?

Because the spider spied 'er!

What do you get if you cross a computer with a million mosquitos?

A gigabyte!

What goes 'snap, crackle and pop'?

A firefly with a short circuit!

What did the spider say when he broke his new web?

"Darn it!"

What did the two spiders say to the fly?

"We're getting married do you want to come to the webbing?"

How do snails get their shells so shiny?

They use snail varnish!

What did the maggot say to his friend when he got stuck in an apple?

"Worm your way out of that one!"

What is life like for a wood worm?

Boring!

Why didn't the two worms get on Noah's Ark in an apple?

Because everyone had to go on in pairs!

What do you get if you cross a rabbit and fleas?

Bugs Bunny!

What is the difference between a flea-bitten dog and a bored visitor?

Ones going to itch and the other is itching to go!

What did one flea say to the other after a night out?

"Shall we walk home or take a dog?"

Two spiders were running across the top of a cereal box. One says to the other, "Why are we running so fast?"

"Because it says tear along the dotted line!"

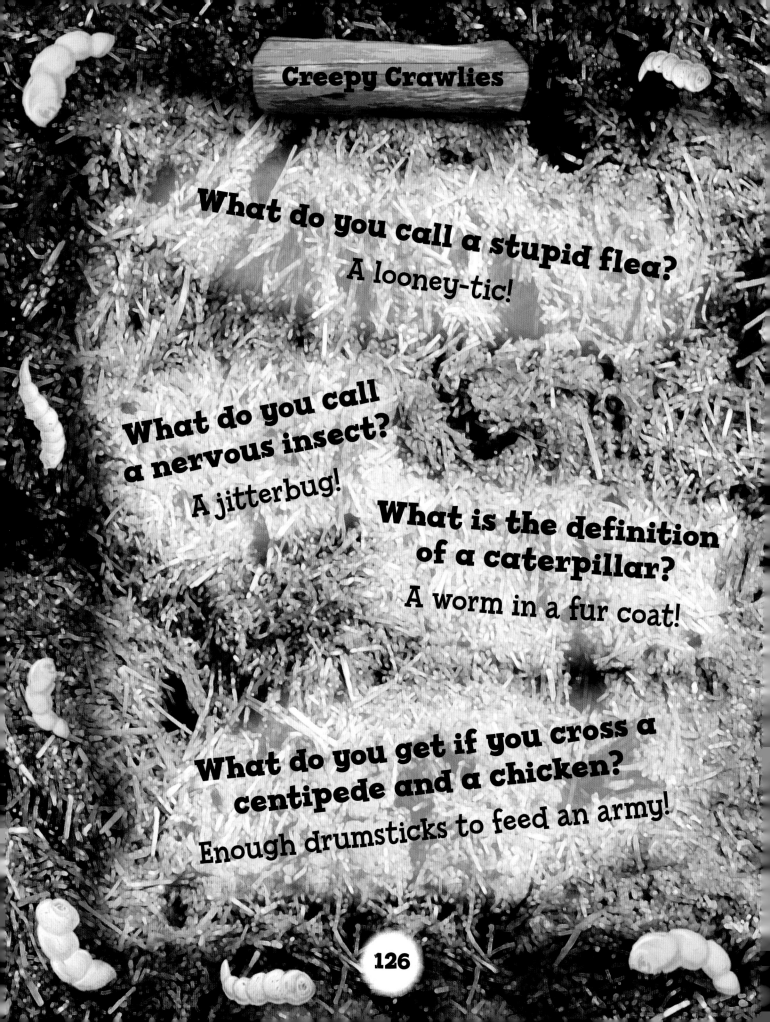

What do you call a stupid flea?

A looney-tic!

What do you call a nervous insect?

A jitterbug!

What is the definition of a caterpillar?

A worm in a fur coat!

What do you get if you cross a centipede and a chicken?

Enough drumsticks to feed an army!

Why was the centipede dropped from the insect football team?

He took too long to put his boots on!

What is green and can jump a mile in a minute?

A grasshopper with hiccups!

Why wouldn't they let the butterfly into the dance?

Because it was a moth ball!

Where would you put an injured insect?

In an ant-bulance!

Sports

Who came last in the Winter Olympics?

The Abominable Slowman!

How do vampire footballers wash?

They all get in the bat tub!

Patient: "Doctor, doctor, I feel like a tennis racquet."

Doctor: "Yes, you do seem highly strung!"

What happened when two huge monsters ran in a race?

One ran in short bursts, the other one ran in burst shorts!

How do ghosts keep fit?

With regular exorcise!

What do you call a non-swimmer who falls in a river?

Bob!

What's sport do vampire's like best?

Bat-minton!

Why did the monster sit on a pumpkin?

It wanted to play squash!

What do you do if you split your sides laughing?

Run until you get a stitch in them!

Why did the ballerina quit?

Because it was tu-tu hard!

Who is the most important member of the ghost's football team?

The ghoulie!

Why did the surfer stop surfing?

Because the sea weed!

Who won the world's strongest vegetable contest?

The muscle sprout!

What do you get if you cross an England footballer with a chicken?

David Peckham!

Who won the vampires' race?

It was neck and neck!

What's the hardest part about skydiving?

The ground!

Why are babies good at basketball?

Because they're great dribblers!

What goes in pink and comes out blue?

A swimmer on a cold day!

Matt: "The teacher said I would be on the football team except for two things."

Dad: "What are they?"

Matt: "My feet!"

Why do basketball players carry hankies around with them?

They are always dribbling!

How did the football pitch turn into a triangle?

Someone took a corner!

If you have a referee in football and an umpire in tennis, what do you have in bowls?

A goldfish!

Which athlete is always warm?

The long jumper!

Why did the midfielder refuse to travel by plane?

He didn't want to be put on the wing!

How do footballers stay cool during the game?

They stand close to the fans!

Why did the monster take two pairs of socks to the golf course?

In case he got a hole-in-one!

What do you get if you cross a martial artist with a pig?

A pork chop!

What do boxers like to drink?

Fruit punch!

What animal is best at hitting a baseball?

A bat!

Did you hear about the crazy monster who wanted to listen to the match?

He burnt his ear!

What lights up a football stadium?

A football match!

Why was the turkey sent off in the football game?

Fowl play!

Did you hear about the ghosts' race?

It was a dead heat!

What do magicians and footballers have in common?

They both do hat tricks!

Why is tennis so noisy?

Every player raises a racquet!

What has five heads, ten legs and is purple?

A basketball team holding their breath!

Did you hear about the monster who exploded during the race?

He bust a gut trying to win!

Tom: "How are you getting on with your trampoline lessons?"

Josh: "Oh, you know, up and down!"

What do monsters play when they are in their mum's car?

Squash!

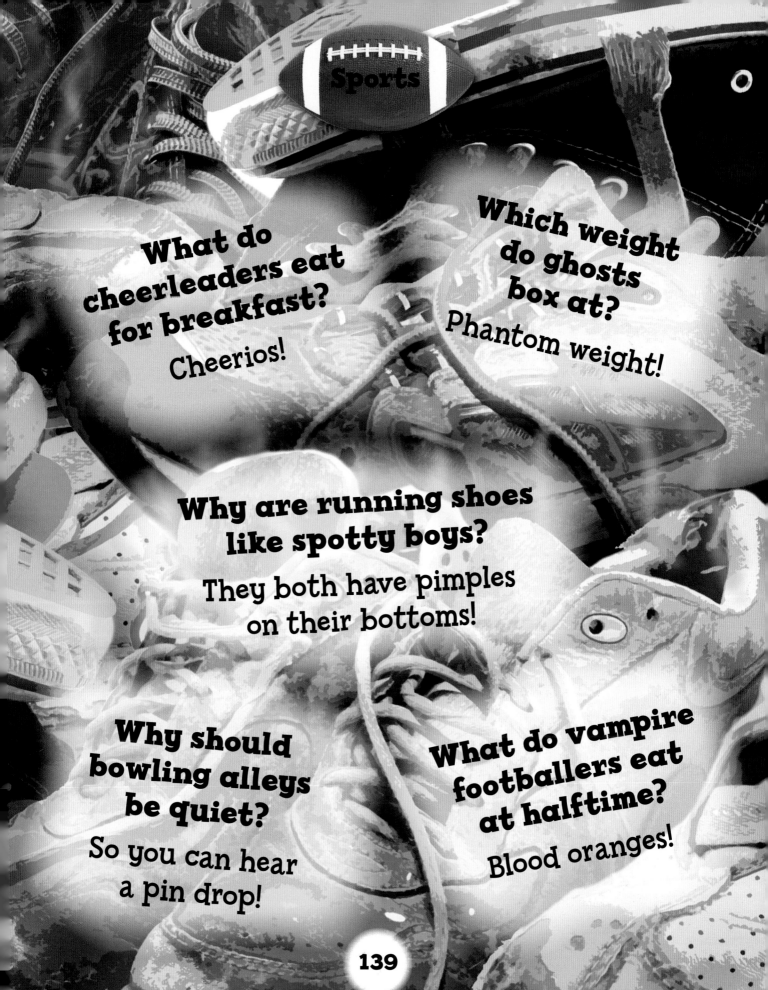

What do cheerleaders eat for breakfast?

Cheerios!

Which weight do ghosts box at?

Phantom weight!

Why are running shoes like spotty boys?

They both have pimples on their bottoms!

Why should bowling alleys be quiet?

So you can hear a pin drop!

What do vampire footballers eat at halftime?

Blood oranges!

A mountaineer got into difficulties when he was dangling from a rope over the edge of a precipice. As his friend began to pull him up, the rope started to fray.

"What will we do if the rope breaks?" asked the man, fearfully.

"Don't worry," called the other man. "I've got another!"

What's the difference between a nail and a boxer?

One gets knocked in, the other gets knocked out!

What did the monster say when he accidentally burped during the match?

"Sorry, it was a freak-hic!"

Why did Richard's rugby team always win?

Their feet smelt so bad that the other teams would never dare tackle them!

Why are fairy godmothers surprisingly good football coaches?

They always help you get to the ball!

What do ghosts say when a girl footballer is sent off?

"Ban-she, ban-she!"

Why can't you tell a joke whilst ice skating?

The ice might crack up!

Why did the basketball player go to the doctor?

To get more shots!

Which animal can jump higher than a house?

All of them. Houses can't jump!

What happened when the martial artist joined the army?

He saluted and knocked himself out!

Why was Cinderella kicked off the football team?

She kept running away from the ball!

Where do fruits play cricket?
On the cricket peach!

Why do footballers make bad dinner dates?
They dribble too much!

Why was Cinderella rubbish at tennis?
Her coach was a pumpkin!

What is the naughtiest sport?
Bad-minton!

Which international cricket team plays half dressed?
The 'Vest' Indies!

How can you swim 100 meters in a few seconds?

Go over a waterfall!

Why was the monster baseball team arrested?

There were reports of a hit and run!

Why was the computer so good at golf?

Because it had a hard drive!

Tom: "You've got your boots on the wrong feet."

Josh: "They're the only feet I've got!"

Why should you never hold a sports day in the jungle?

There are too many cheetahs!

Why didn't the dog want to play football?

It was a boxer!

How long does it take to learn to ice skate?

A few sittings!

Did you hear about the stinky footballer?

He was scent off!

Why do basketball players love donuts?

Because they dunk them!

Manager: "Richard, why have you brought a broom to football practice?"

Richard: "You said I was going to play sweeper!"

What time of year is it best to jump on a trampoline?

Spring!

What game do wizard octopuses play?

Squid-ditch!

What song do cross-channel swimmers always sing?

"Please re-grease me!"

What do monster runners do when they forget something?

They jog their memory!

Why was the ball dribbling?

You'd dribble too if your head was bouncing off the floor!

Did you hear about the tap dancer?

He fell into the sink!

What runs around a football pitch but doesn't move?

A fence!

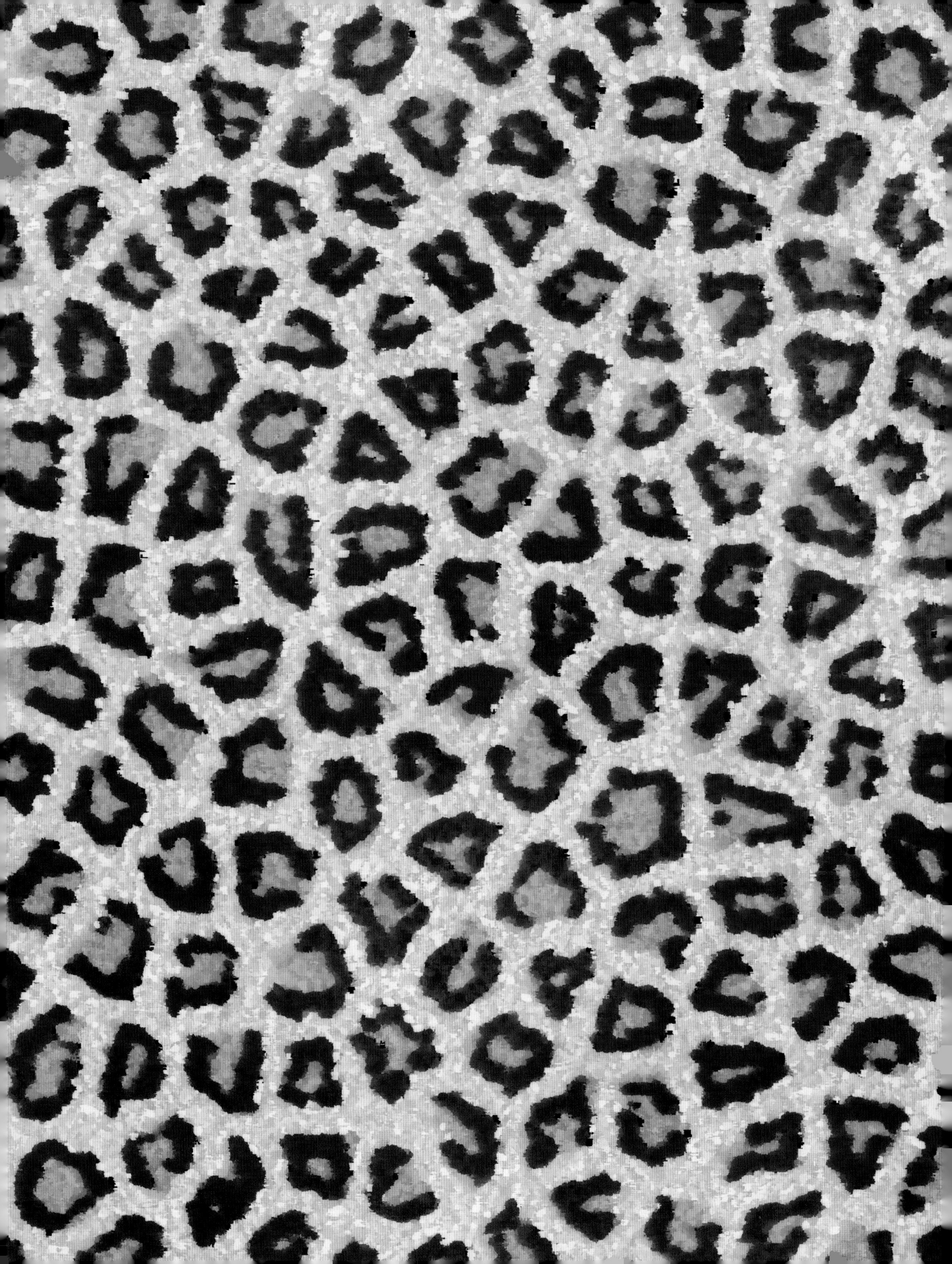

Animals

What's green and goes round at 100 miles an hour?

A frog in a washing machine!

What do cats have for a Friday night treat?

Special fried mice!

What's small, cuddly and bright purple?

A koala holding its breath!

What did the bear eat when he had toothache?

The dentist!

What do you give an elephant that's going to be sick?

Plenty of space!

What do you get if you cross a cow with a camel?

Lumpy milkshakes!

What do you call a bear with its ear cut off?

B!

What's yellow, sticky and smells of bananas?

Monkey sick!

Why aren't elephants allowed on beaches?

They can't keep their trunks up!

How do you find where a flea has bitten you?

Start from scratch!

What do cats put in their lemonade?

Mice cubes!

What do you get if you cross a duck with a firework?

A fire-quacker!

What do you get when you cross a cow with a grass cutter?

A lawn moo-er!

What's bright red and weighs four tons?

An elephant with a knot in its trunk!

What do you get if you cross a skunk and an owl?

A bird that smells, but doesn't give a hoot!

What's big, grey and wears a mask?

The Ele-phantom of the Opera!

What do you call a frozen cat?

A cat-cicle!

Farmer: "I had to shoot the cow."

Farmer's wife: "Was he mad?"

Farmer: "He wasn't too happy about it!"

What do camels wear on hunting trips?

Camel-flage!

Is chicken soup good for you?

Not if you're a chicken!

What is a running chicken called?

Poultry in motion!

Why are elephants wrinkly?

Because they don't fit on the ironing board!

What's pink and hard?

A flamingo wearing knuckle dusters!

What do you call a sleeping bull?

A bull-dozer!

What do you call a baby whale?

A little squirt!

What's black, white and noisy?

A zebra with a drum kit!

What do you call a frog with no back legs?

Unhoppy!

What's blue and has big ears?

An elephant at the North Pole!

How do you make a gorilla cross?

Nail two together!

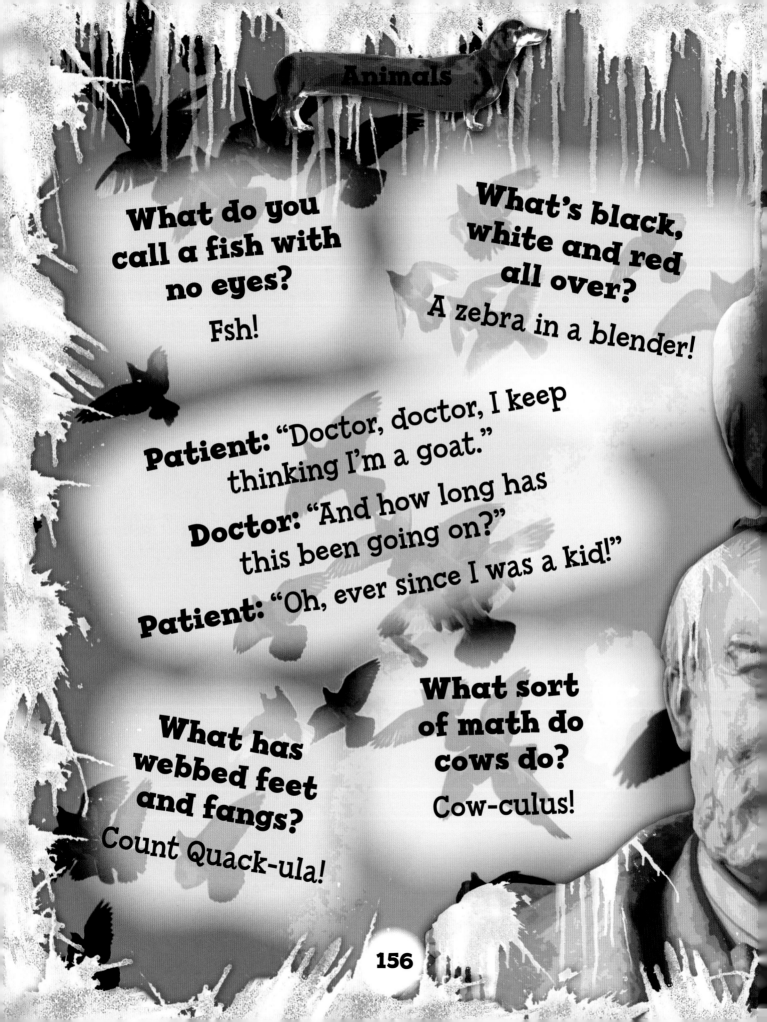

What do you call a fish with no eyes?

Fsh!

What's black, white and red all over?

A zebra in a blender!

Patient: "Doctor, doctor, I keep thinking I'm a goat."

Doctor: "And how long has this been going on?"

Patient: "Oh, ever since I was a kid!"

What has webbed feet and fangs?

Count Quack-ula!

What sort of math do cows do?

Cow-culus!

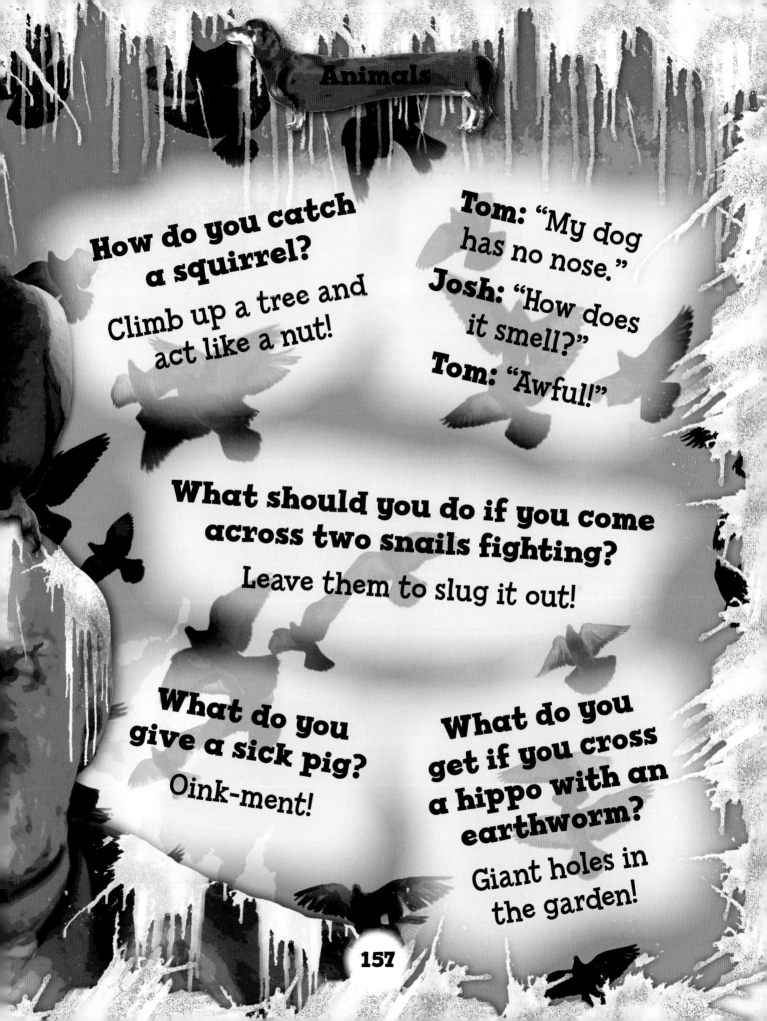

How do you catch a squirrel?

Climb up a tree and act like a nut!

Tom: "My dog has no nose."

Josh: "How does it smell?"

Tom: "Awful!"

What should you do if you come across two snails fighting?

Leave them to slug it out!

What do you give a sick pig?

Oink-ment!

What do you get if you cross a hippo with an earthworm?

Giant holes in the garden!

What is a crocodile's favourite game?

Snap!

What do you call a cow with no legs?

Ground beef!

What's big and hairy and sits in the corner facing the wall?

A naughty gorilla!

Why can't Bob ride a bike?

Because Bob's a fish!

What do you call a lamb with a machine gun?

Lamb-o!

What do you call an elephant that never washes?

A smelly-phant!

Where does Superman's goldfish live?

In a superbowl!

Why is it difficult to eat chocolate moose?

The antlers get stuck in your throat!

What do you do when an elephant sneezes?

Run!

Which animal has the biggest bum?

A hippo-bottomus!

What do you do if you find a poisonous snake in your toilet ?

Wait till he's finished!

What do you get if you cross a parrot with a seagull?

A bird that makes a mess on your head, then apologizes!

Tom: "Our parrot lays square eggs."

Josh: "Does it talk?"

Tom: "Yes, but it can only say one word."

Josh: "What's that?"

Tom: "Ouch!"

What do you call a gorilla with bananas in his ears?

Anything, he can't hear you!

What do you get if you cross a cow, a sheep and a goat?

The milky-baa kid!

What are crisp, like milk and go 'eek, eek, eek' when you eat them?

Mice Krispies!

What's invisible and smells of bananas?

Monkey farts!

Why did the chameleon have a nervous breakdown?

He was sat on a tartan rug!

What's big and grey and squirts green gunk at you?

An elephant with the flu!

What happens when a cat licks a lemon?

It turns into a sour puss!

What has six eyes but cannot see?

Three blind mice!

What do you call a pig with no clothes on?

Streaky bacon!

What do you get if you cross a science fiction film with a toad?

Star Warts!

How do hedgehogs play leap-frog?

Very carefully!

How can you tell when a moth farts?

It flies in a straight line for a second!

What wears a coat all summer and pants all winter?

A dog!

What's invisible and smells of nuts?

Squirrel farts!

What do you call a headless sheep with no legs?

A cloud!

What do you call a pig that does karate?

Pork chop!

Little birdie flying high, dropped a message from the sky...

... "Oh," said the farmer, wiping his eye, "it's a good job that cows can't fly!"

What do you get if you feed gunpowder to a chicken?

An egg-splosion!

What do you get if you cross a chicken with a cement mixer?

A brick layer!

Why did the farmer give his chickens whisky?

He wanted scotch eggs!

How do you con sheep?

Pull the wool over their eyes!

What do you get if you cross some nuns with a chicken?

A pecking order!

What do you call a three-legged ass?

A wonkey donkey!

How do you make ice-cream?

Put a cow in the freezer!

Which animal has a lot of gas?

An aard-fart!

What did the leopard say after he had devoured a gazelle?

"That hit the spots!"

What is out of bounds?

A tired kangaroo!

What do you call a rubbish lion tamer?

Claude B. Hinde!

What smells like eucalyptus?

Koala farts!

What sort of dog has no tail and no legs?

A hot dog!

What do you get if you cross a bird with a snake?

A feather boa!

What goes 'ha, ha, ha, plop'?

A hyena laughing its head off!

Why did the stag wear braces?

He had buck teeth!

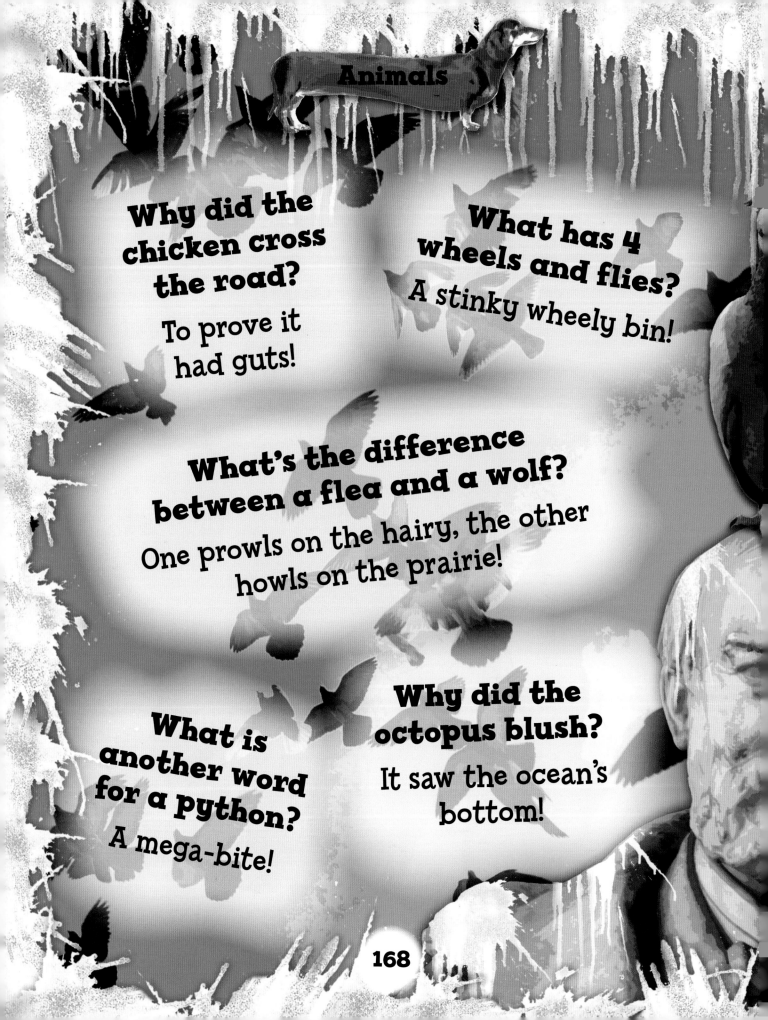

Why did the chicken cross the road?

To prove it had guts!

What has 4 wheels and flies?

A stinky wheely bin!

What's the difference between a flea and a wolf?

One prowls on the hairy, the other howls on the prairie!

What is another word for a python?

A mega-bite!

Why did the octopus blush?

It saw the ocean's bottom!

Josh: "I keep a pig under my bed."

Tom: "What about the smell?"

Josh: "He doesn't mind!"

Why do elephants stomp on people?

They like the squishy feeling between their toes!

What do you get if you cross a jellyfish with an elephant?

Jelly the elephant!

What goes eek, eek, bang?

A mouse in a minefield!

What did the monkey do when he lost his tail?

He went to the re-tailer!

How does a bird with a broken wing land safely?

With a sparrow-chute!

Why do gorillas have big nostrils?

Because they have big fingers!

Patient: "Doctor, doctor, I keep thinking I'm a sheep."

Doctor: "Really? And how do you feel about that?"

Patient: "Very baaaaaaad!"

What's green, slimy and drips from trees?

Giraffe bogies!

Why do birds fly south for the winter?

It's too far to walk!

Where does a horse go when he gets sick?

The horse-pital!

Did you hear about the sunburnt shark?

He was basking for it!

"Doctor doctor, I feel like a frog. I'm afraid I could croak at any moment!"

What type of fish performs operations?

A sturgeon!

What do you call a woodpecker with no beak?

A headbanger!

What do you get it you cross a piranha and a nose?

I don't know, but I wouldn't pick it!

What has two grey legs and two brown legs?

A hippopotamus with diarrhea!

Jason: "I've just been thrown out of the zoo for feeding the monkeys."

Lauren: "What? Why?"

Jason: "I fed them to the lions!"

What is dry on the outside, filled with water and blows up buildings?

A fish tank!

Why was the crab not very good at sharing?

He was shell-fish!

Why are skunks always arguing?

Because they like to raise a stink!

What happens when you put a mouse in the freezer?

You get mice cubes!

Why do giraffes have such long necks?

Have you ever smelt a giraffe fart?

What kind of snake is good at maths?

An adder!

Did you hear about the dog that lay down to eat a bone?

When it stood up it only had three legs!

How many skunks does it take to make a big stink?

A phew!

What did the farmer call the cow that would not give him any milk?

An udder disgrace!

Why did the pig go to the casino?

To play the slop machines!

What do you call a girl with a frog in her hair?

Lily!

What's yellow and goes round at 100 miles an hour?

A mouldy frog in a washing machine!

What do you give a pony with a cold?

Cough-stirrup!

How did the pig get to hospital?

In a ham-bulance!

What clothes do fleas wear to work?

Jump suits!

What kind of creature is made out of wood?

A timber wolf!

What happened when the cow jumped over the barbed-wire fence?

It was an udder catastrophe!

What do you call a donkey with one eye and three legs?

A winky wonky donkey!

What happens when you cross a girl jellyfish and a boy jellyfish?

Jelly babies!

What do you get when a cow gets caught in an earthquake?

Milkshake!

What was written on the turkey's gravestone?

Roast in peace!

What do you call a cow that can go in the washing machine?

Washer-bull!

What do you get if you cross a pig with a centipede?

Bacon and legs!

What type of dog runs away from frying pans?

A sausage dog!

What was the canary doing in prison?

It was a jailbird!

What do you call a row of rabbits walking backwards?

A receding hare line!

How do you know when your cat's eaten a duck?

It looks down in the mouth!

Why do cats have fur balls?

Because they love a good gag!

What do you call a dog with a cold?

Achoo-huahua!

What do you give a dog with a temperature?

Mustard – it's the best thing for a hot dog!

What happened when the dog went to the flea circus?

It stole the show!

What do you call a dog that digs up bones?

A barky-ologist!

What do you call a mouse with no legs?

Cat food!

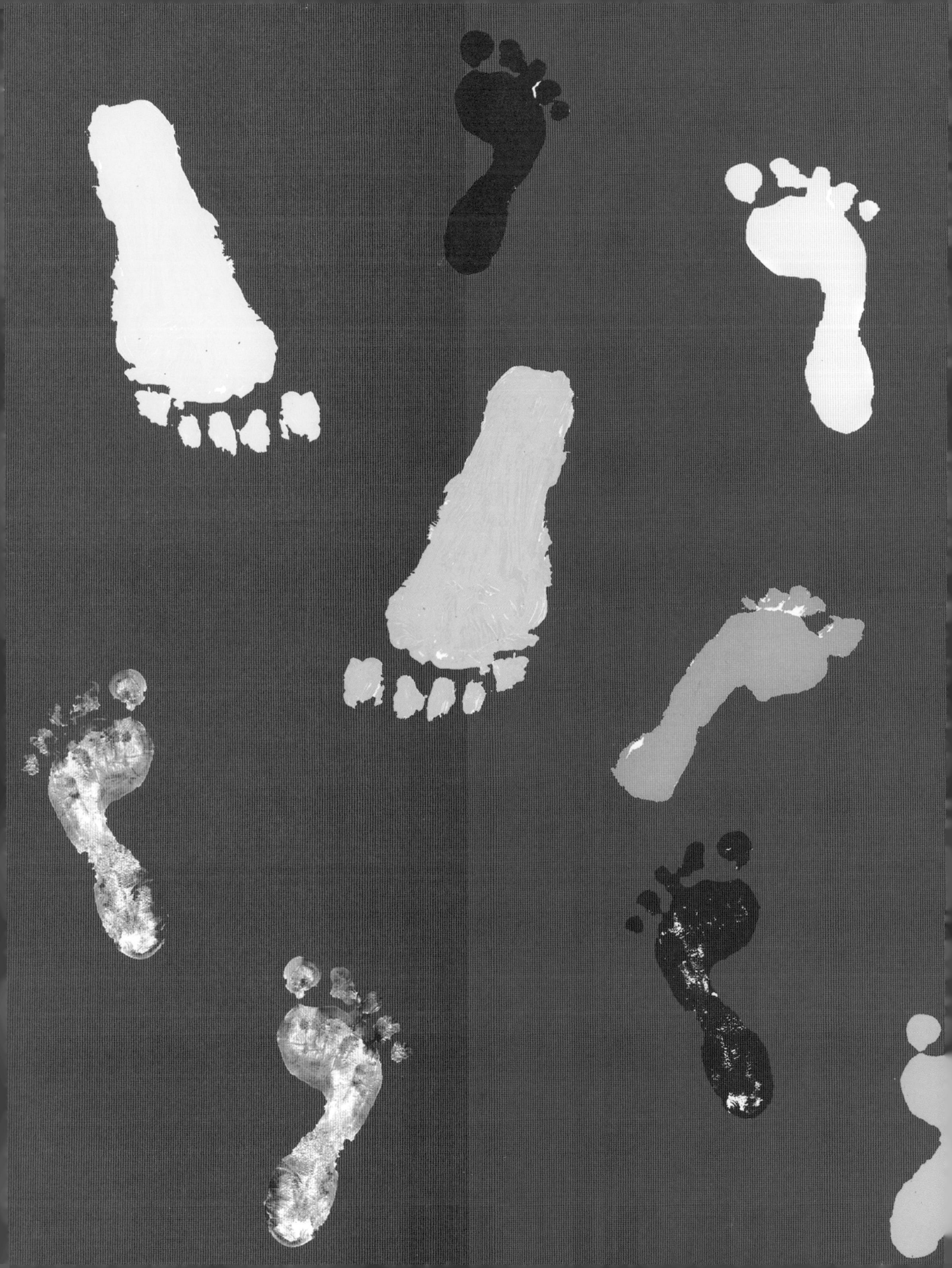

Human Body

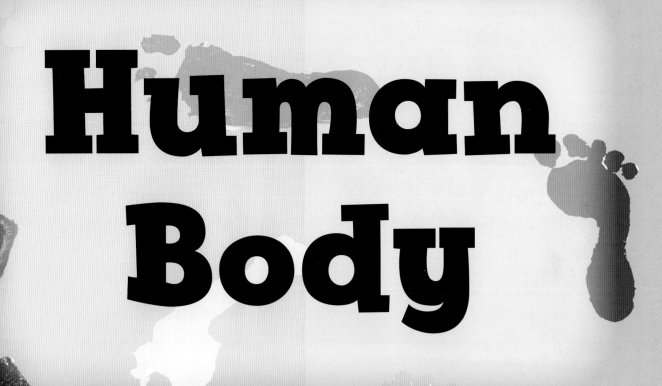

Patient: "Doctor, doctor, I keep thinking I'm a toilet!"

Doctor: "I thought you were looking rather flushed!"

How can you cure a headache?

Put your head through the window and the pane will disappear!

Tom: "What do you clean your top teeth with?"

Josh: "A toothbrush?"

Tom: "And?"

Josh: "Toothpaste."

Tom: "And what about your bottom?"

Josh: "The same."

Tom: "Eurgh! That's disgusting, I use toilet paper!"

Why did the sword-swallower switch to pins and needles?

He needed to lose weight!

Did you hear about the plastic surgeon?

He sat by the fire and melted!

Patient: "Doctor, doctor, I've got a strawberry stuck up my bum."
Doctor: "I've got some cream for that!"

What do you get if someone hits you on the head with an axe?

A splitting headache!

What's bright red and stupid?
A blood clot!

How can you cure dandruff?
Cut off your head!

Patient: "Doctor, doctor, I'm scared. This is my first operation."
Doctor: "I know how you feel, it's my first one, too!"

What has a bottom at its top?
A leg!

What should you do if your nose goes on strike?
Picket!

What do you say to a one-legged hitch hiker?

"Hop in!"

What do you call a judge with no thumbs?

Justice Fingers!

Lauren: "My beauty is timeless."

Jason: "Yes, it could stop clocks!"

What do surgeons do with their mistakes?

Bury them!

What has two legs but can't walk?

A pair of jeans!

What can you keep and give to someone else at the same time?

The flu!

When is it wrong to bury people in a graveyard?

When they're still alive!

Knock, knock.

Who's there?

Juliet.

Juliet who?

Juliet so many sausages she feels ill!

Patient: "Doctor, doctor, you've taken out my tonsils, my adenoids, my gall bladder, my varicose veins and my appendix, but I still don't feel well."

Doctor: "That's quite enough out of you!"

I never forget a face, but in your case I'll make an exception!

Patient: "Doctor, doctor, I'm at death's door!"
Doctor: "Don't worry, I'll pull you through!"

An old man and his wife were sitting in a library. The old man said, "I just let out a silent fart. What should I do?"
His wife said, "Well for one thing you should change your hearing aid battery!"

Tom: "Our teacher has a sympathetic face."
Josh: "What do you mean?"
Tom: "People look at her and feel sympathy!"

What do you call a nun with a washing machine on her head?

Sister-Matic!

What happened to the boy who swallowed a torch?

He hiccupped with delight!

What man never gets his hair wet in the shower?

A bald one!

What do you call a woman with only one tooth?

Peg!

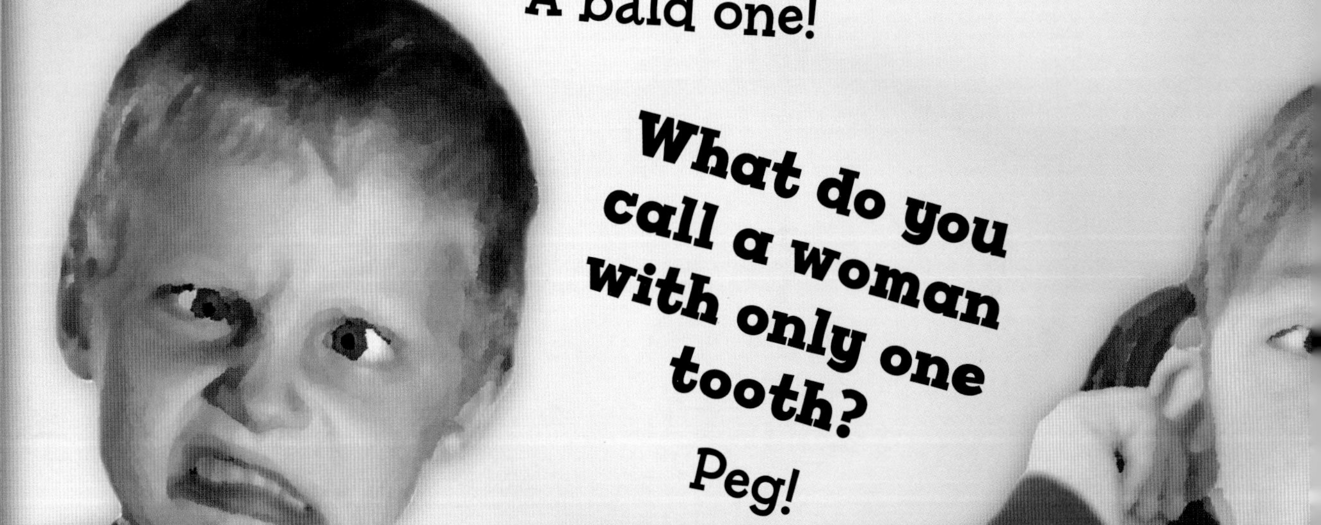

Sarah: "Why aren't you taking Jake to the prom? I thought you said it was love at first sight."

Lisa: "It was the second and third viewings that put me off!"

Patient: "Doctor, doctor, I keep thinking I'm a pool ball."

Doctor: "Get to the end of the queue!"

Did the native Americans hunt bear?

Not in the winter!

What do children and gardeners have in common?

They both have green fingers!

What does a boy do when a girl rolls her eyes at him?

Rolls them back!

Surgeon: "I'm afraid we have good news and bad news: the bad news is that we've had to take off both your feet. The good news is that the man in the next bed wants to buy your slippers!"

Knock, knock.

Who's there?

Ivor.

Ivor who?

Ivor a spot on my bum!

What kind of monster gets up your nose?

The bogey-man!

Patient: "Doctor, doctor, what does this X-ray of my head show?"

Doctor: "Unfortunately, nothing!"

Why did the crazy undertaker chop all his corpses into tiny bits?

He wanted them to rest in pieces!

What should you do with rotten nails?

Save them in a nail file!

What has ears, but can't hear?

Corn!

Patient: "Doctor, doctor, my mind keeps wandering."

Doctor: "Don't worry – it's too weak to go very far!"

What happened when the girl found out her boyfriend had a wooden leg?

She broke it off!

Why did the thief saw his legs off?

He wanted to lie low!

What do you call a sleep-walking nun?

A roaming catholic!

Patient: "Doctor, doctor, I can't stop sneezing."

Doctor: "Don't worry - it's much achoo about nothing!"

What's the difference between a thermometer that goes up your bottom, and one that goes in your mouth?

The taste!

What did one tonsil say to the other?

"Get dressed. The doctor's taking us out tonight!"

What might you win if you lose ten kilos?

The Nobel-ly Prize!

Why did the sword-swallower swallow an umbrella?

He wanted to put something away for a rainy day!

Patient: Doctor, doctor, I've developed a double heart beat since my operation.

Doctor: Ah, so that's where my wristwatch went!

Where does an undertaker work?

In a box office!

How can you stop your nose running?

Stick out your foot and trip it up!

Tom: "This morning I put soap flakes in my brother's cornflakes."

Josh: "What happened?"

Tom: "He got so mad, he was foaming at the mouth!"

Patient: "Doctor, doctor, I keep breaking wind. Is there anything you can suggest?"

Doctor: "Yes, take up wind surfing!"

How do you know if someone has a glass eye?

It comes out in conversation!

Why did the sword-swallower only swallow half a sword?

He was having a mid-knife crisis!

Sarah: "Dad, there's a man with a beard at the door."

Dad: "Tell him I already have one!"

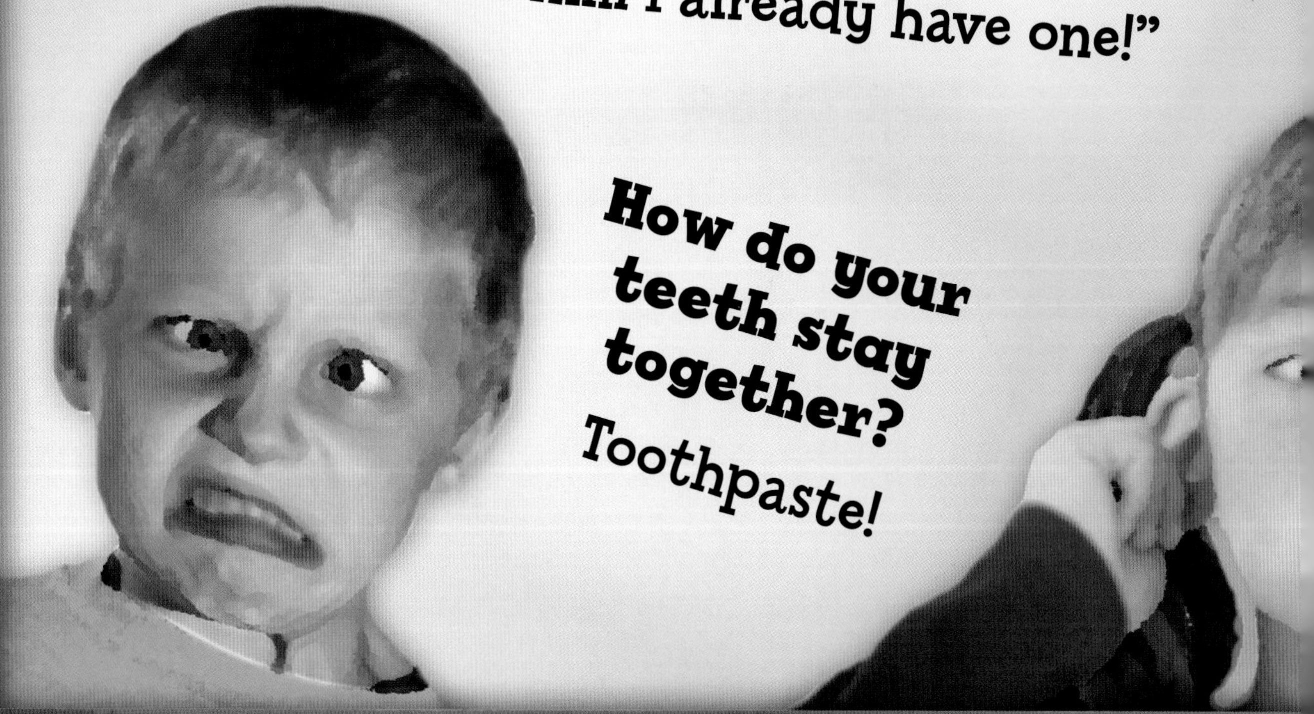

How do your teeth stay together?

Toothpaste!

What did one crash test dummy say to the other crash test dummy?

"Can I crash at your place tonight?"

Patient: "Doctor, doctor, I've swallowed a roll of film."

Doctor: "Sit in a darkened room and we'll see what develops!"

What did one bogey say to another?

"You think you're funny, but you're snot!"

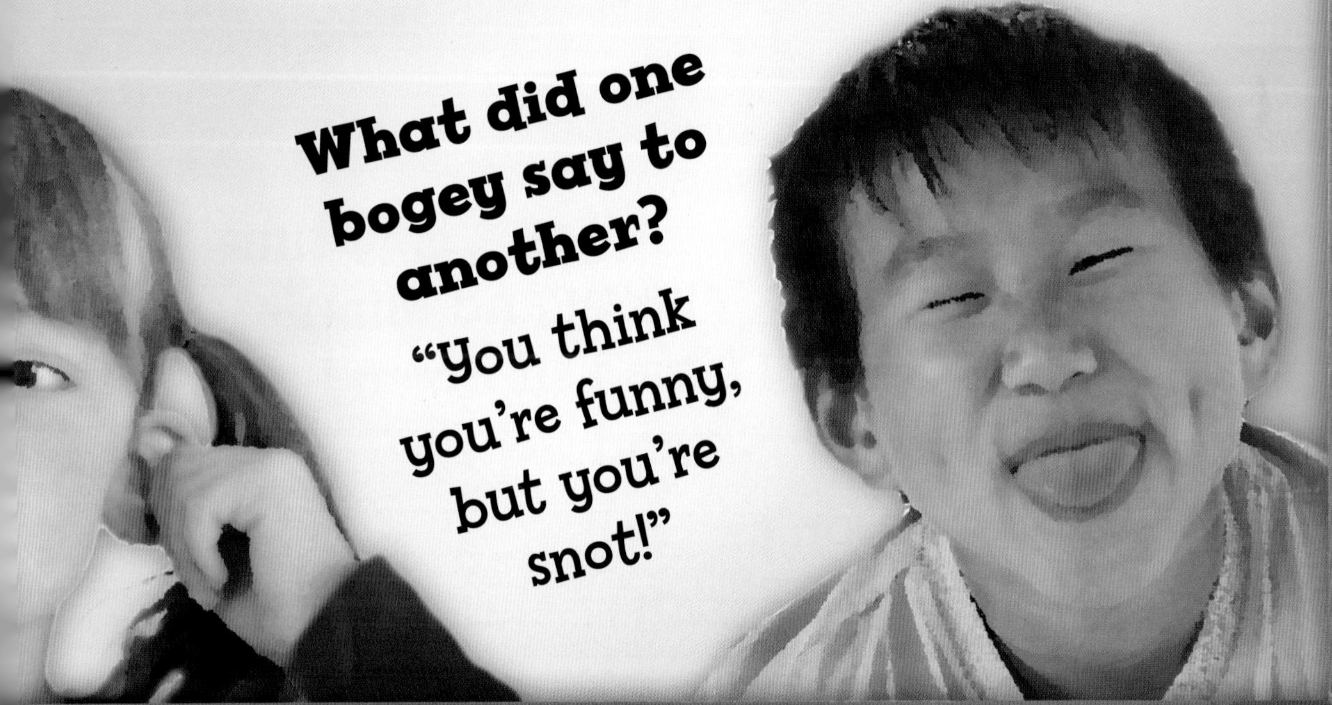

Why were the Baker's hands brown and sticky?

Because he kneaded a poo!

Knock, knock.

Who's there?

Dishes.

Dishes who?

Dishes the way I talk now I've got false teeth!

Patient: "Doctor, doctor, every time I stand up I see Mickey and Minnie Mouse and every time I sit down I see Donald Duck and Goofy."

Doctor: "Don't worry, you're just having Disney spells!"

Why did the monster take his nose apart?

To see what made it run!

Did you hear the joke about the chiropodist?

It's kind of corny!

Patient: "Doctor, doctor, will my measles be gone by the weekend?"
Doctor: "I don't want to make any rash promises!"

What did the bald man say when he received a comb for his birthday?

"Thanks, I'll never part with it!"

Why did the angel go to the doctor?

She had harp failure!

How did the man feel after he got run over?

Tyred!

Patient: "Doctor, doctor, I feel like a piano."

Doctor: "I'd better make some notes!"

What do people with weak bladders and people who wear old stockings have in common?

They both get runs down their legs!

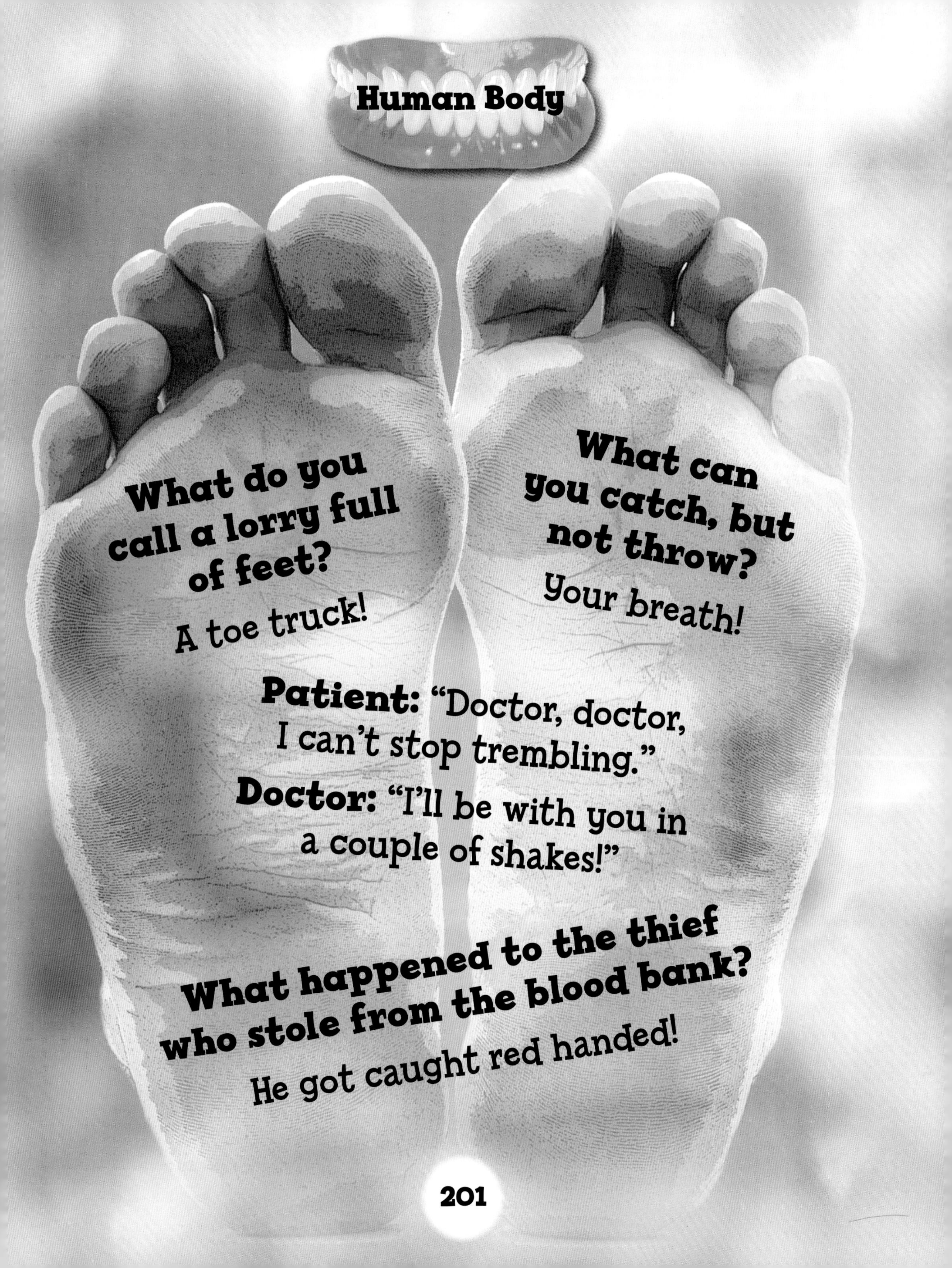

What do you call a lorry full of feet?

A toe truck!

What can you catch, but not throw?

Your breath!

Patient: "Doctor, doctor, I can't stop trembling."

Doctor: "I'll be with you in a couple of shakes!"

What happened to the thief who stole from the blood bank?

He got caught red handed!

Why did the undertaker's son not want to follow in his father's footsteps?

He thought it was a dead end job!

What grows between your nose and your chin?

Two-lips!

Josh: "Dad, how old are you?"

Dad: "41, but I don't look it do I?"

Josh: "No, you used to!"

Patient: "Doctor, doctor, my eyes keep falling out. Can you give me something to keep them in?"

Doctor: "How about this plastic bag?"

What do you call a lady with one leg shorter than the other?

Eileen!

Did you hear about the stupid couple that got frostbite at the drive-in movie?

They went to see 'Closed for Winter'!

Lauren: "Richard is off school because Sarah broke an arm."

Jason: "Well why is Richard off school if Sarah broke an arm?"

Lauren: "It was his arm she broke!"

Why did the secretary cut her fingers off?

So she could do short hand!

Patient: "Doctor, doctor, I just swallowed a bone."

Doctor: "Are you choking?"

Patient: "No, I'm being serious!"

Patient: "Doctor, doctor, I have a hoarse throat."

Doctor: "The resemblance doesn't stop there!"

How do you know if you're upside down?

Your nose runs and your feet smell!

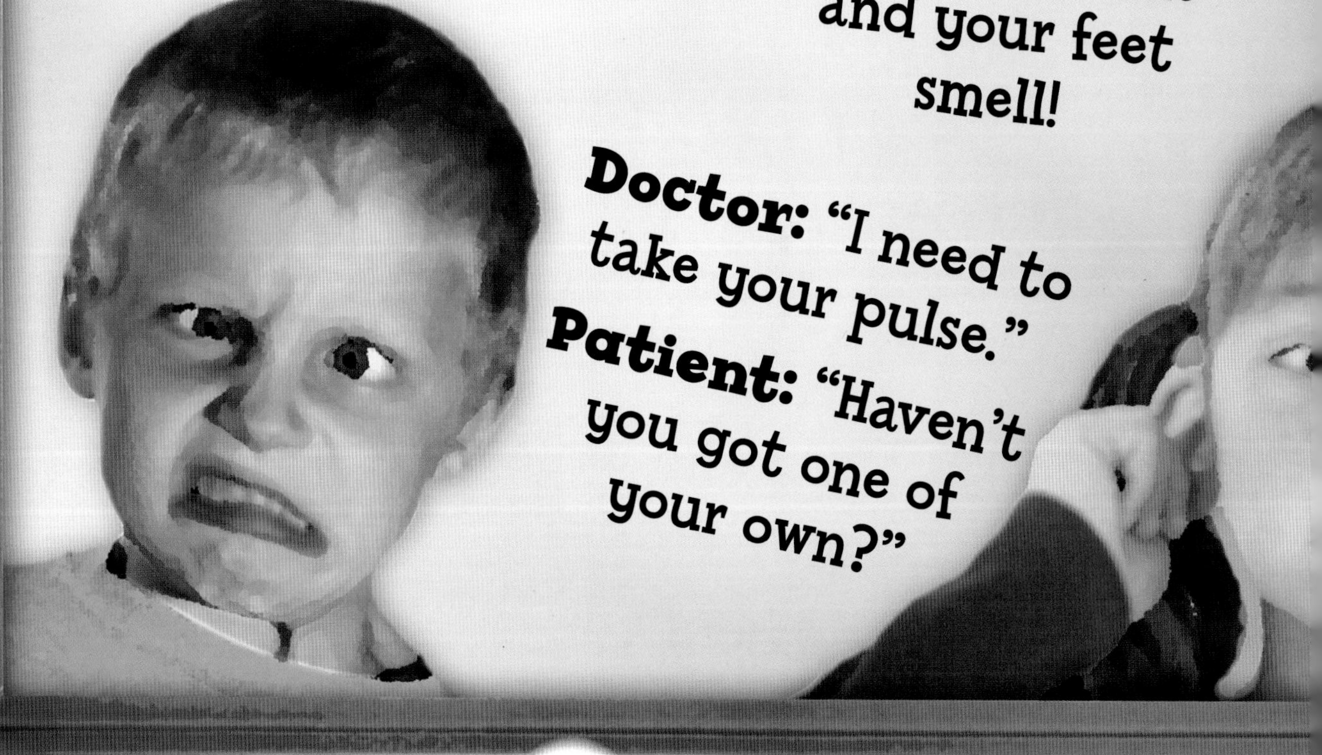

Doctor: "I need to take your pulse."

Patient: "Haven't you got one of your own?"

Patient: "Doctor, doctor, I think I've been bitten by a vampire."

Doctor: "Drink this water."

Patient: "Will it make me better?"

Doctor: "No, but I want to see if your neck leaks!"

Craig: "What are you taking for that cough?"

Sarah: "How much will you give me for it?"

What stands in New York and sneezes all day?

The a-choo of liberty!

How can you stop a head cold becoming a chest cold?

Tie a knot in your neck!

Knock, knock.

Who's there?

Watson.

Watson who?

Watson on your nose, it's gross!

Patient: "Doctor, doctor, I'm going bald, is there any cure?"

Doctor: "Yes, smear poo on your head every morning."

Patient: "And that will stop my hair falling out?"

Doctor: "No, but nobody will come near enough to you to notice you're bald!"

What does a dentist call her X-rays?

Tooth-pics!

Patient: "Doctor, doctor, I've got a terrible cough."

Doctor: "Then you should practice more!"

Tom: "If I had 30 pineapples in one hand and 30 pineapples in the other hand, what would I have?"

Josh: "Enormous hands!"

Bar of soap: "Sometimes I think I have the worst job in the world."

Toilet paper: "Think again!"

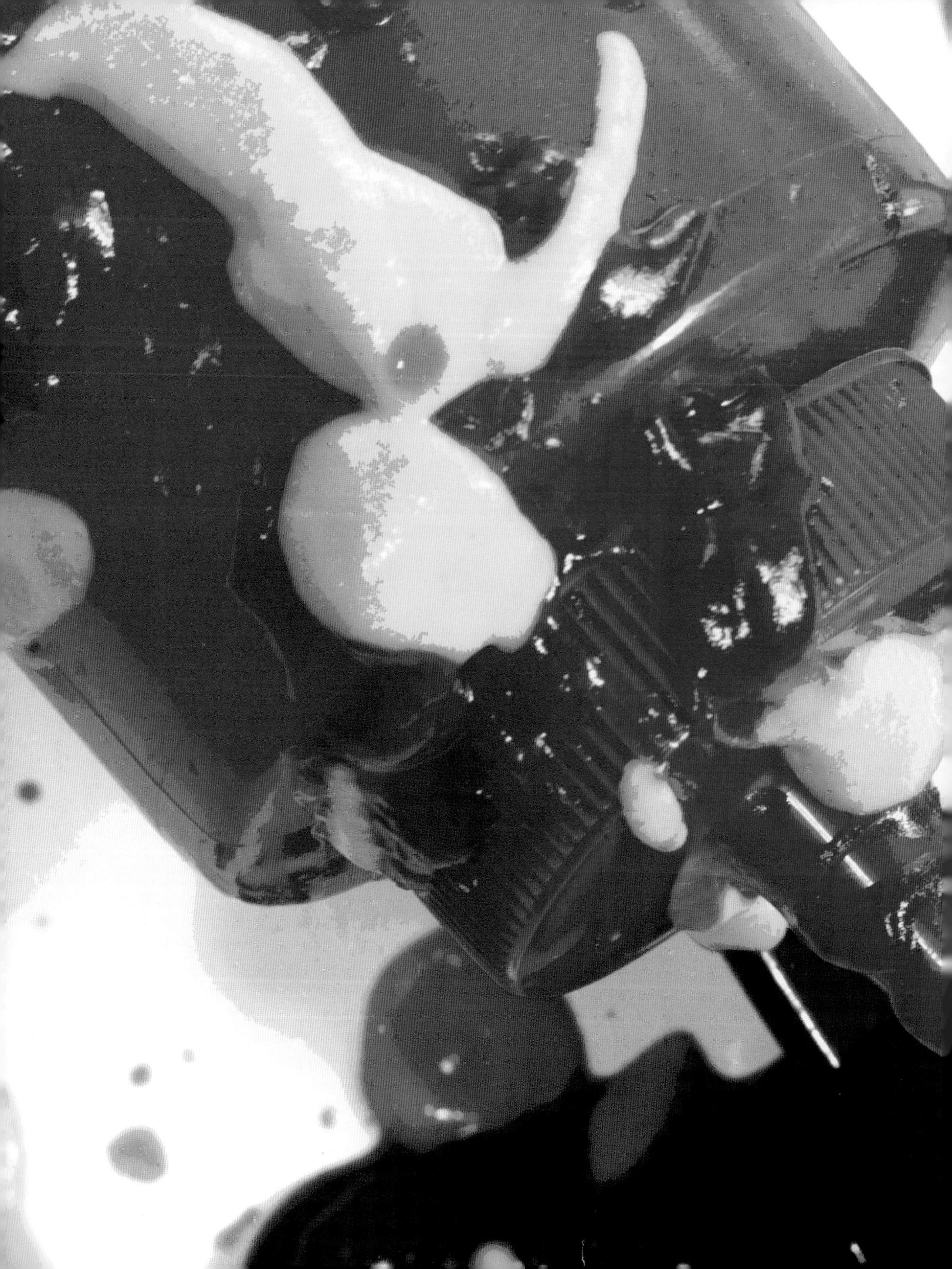

Food

What's the Pied Piper's preferred dinner?

Rat-atouie!

What's the difference between cabbage and bogies?

Kids like to eat bogies!

What's the difference between a fried egg and pea soup?

You can fry an egg, but you can't pea soup!

Peter: "What are you going to do with all that manure?

John: "I'm going to put it on my strawberries."

Peter: "Yuck! I put sugar and cream on mine!"

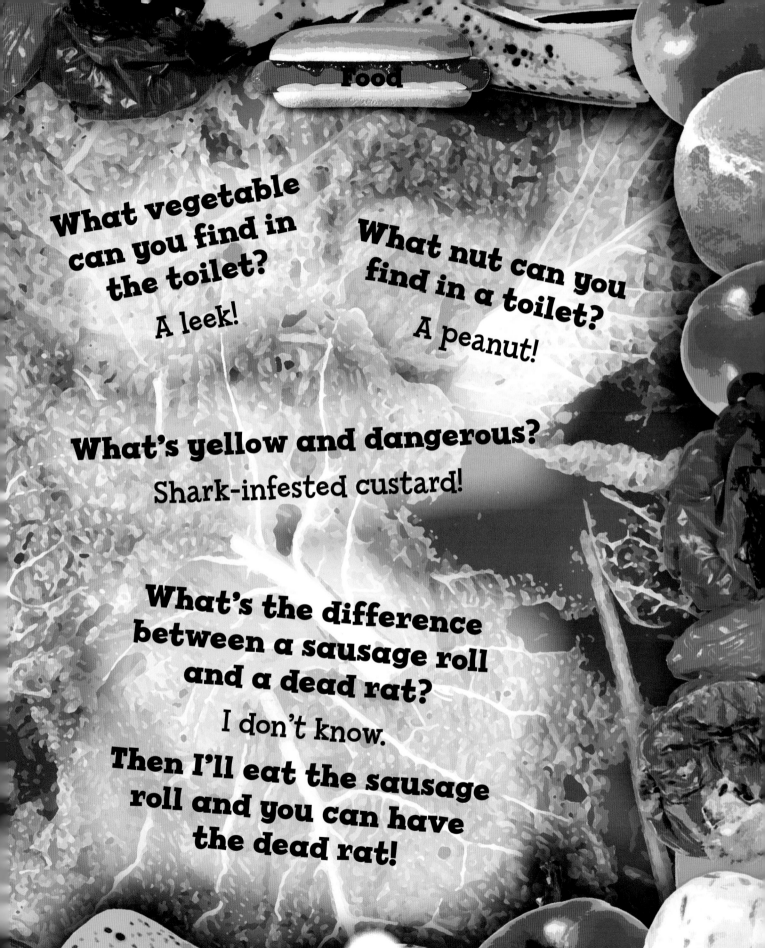

What vegetable can you find in the toilet?

A leek!

What nut can you find in a toilet?

A peanut!

What's yellow and dangerous?

Shark-infested custard!

What's the difference between a sausage roll and a dead rat?

I don't know.

Then I'll eat the sausage roll and you can have the dead rat!

Why are fried onions like a photocopier?

They keep repeating themselves!

What do zombies eat with bread and cheese?

Pickled organs!

Why were the peppers red?

They saw the salad dressing!

Why were the tomatoes red?

Because the greengrocer told them rude stories!

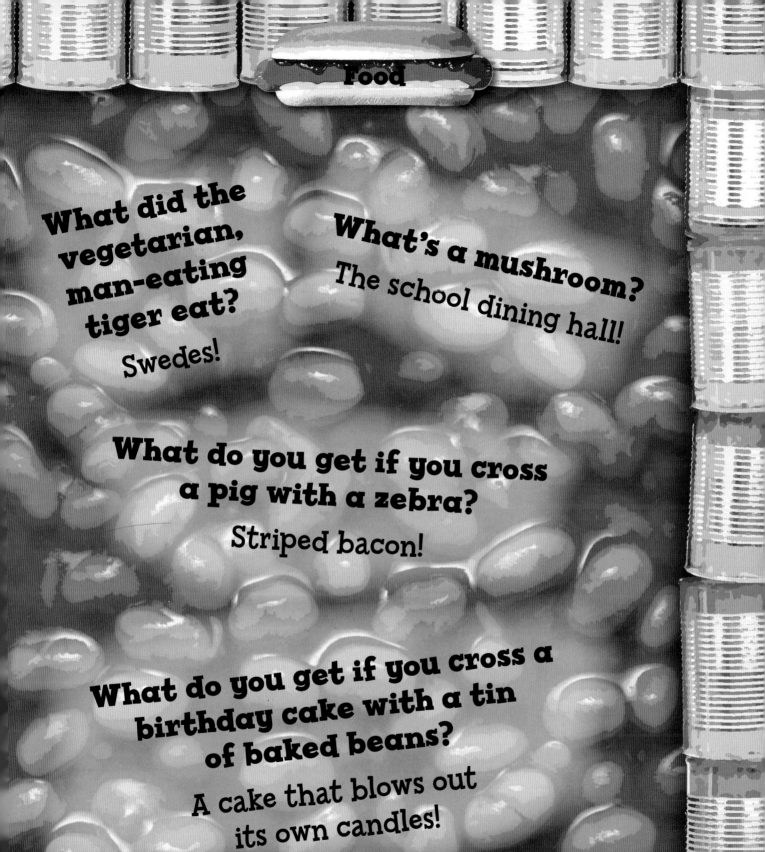

What did the vegetarian, man-eating tiger eat?

Swedes!

What's a mushroom?

The school dining hall!

What do you get if you cross a pig with a zebra?

Striped bacon!

What do you get if you cross a birthday cake with a tin of baked beans?

A cake that blows out its own candles!

What soup do witches eat?

Scream of chicken!

Why did Gary eat little bits of metal all day?

It was his staple diet!

How can you stop fish going bad on Monday?

Eat it on Sunday!

What's yellow, brown and hairy?

Cheese on toast dropped on the carpet!

What did the sausage say as it was about to be put on a skewer?

"Oh spear me, spear me!"

What do you get if you cross a dog with an omelet?

Pooched eggs!

What did one onion say to the other?

"How did we get into this pickle?"

What fish tastes good with ice cream?

Jelly-fish!

I had a dream I ate a giant marshmallow last night...

... I woke up without a pillow!

Patient: "Doctor, doctor, I keep thinking I'm a fruitcake."

Doctor: "What's got into you?"

Patient: "Raisins, cherries, flour..."

Why do sausages have such bad manners?

They spit in the frying pan!

Sarah was feeling seasick on her cruise when the waiter asked if she would like some lunch.

"No thanks," she replied, "just throw it overboard and save me the trouble!"

Patient: "Doctor, doctor, I've got a carrot growing out of my ear."

Doctor: "That's amazing."

Patient: "I know, I planted potatoes in there!"

Patient: "Doctor, doctor, I feel like an apple."

Doctor: "We must get to the core of this!"

What do you call a woman who has toast on her head?

Marge!

Patient: "Doctor, doctor, every time I drink hot chocolate I get a sharp pain in my eye."

Doctor: "Try taking the spoon out before you drink it!"

Patient: "Doctor, doctor, I feel like an apple."
Doctor: "Well come closer, I don't bite!"

"Waiter, there's a fly in my soup!"
"Not to worry sir, the spider in your salad will get it!"

What's round, white, stinky and giggly?
A tickled onion!

Patient: "Doctor, doctor, I feel like a raspberry."
Doctor: "Well I can see you're in a jam!"

What do you call cheese that isn't yours?

Nacho cheese!

"Waiter, your thumb is in my soup!"

"Don't worry sir, it's not hot!"

What's the definition of a balanced diet?

The same amount of cookies in each hand!

Why did the cookie go to the doctor?

It felt crumby!

What do you give a badly injured lemon?

Lemon-aid!

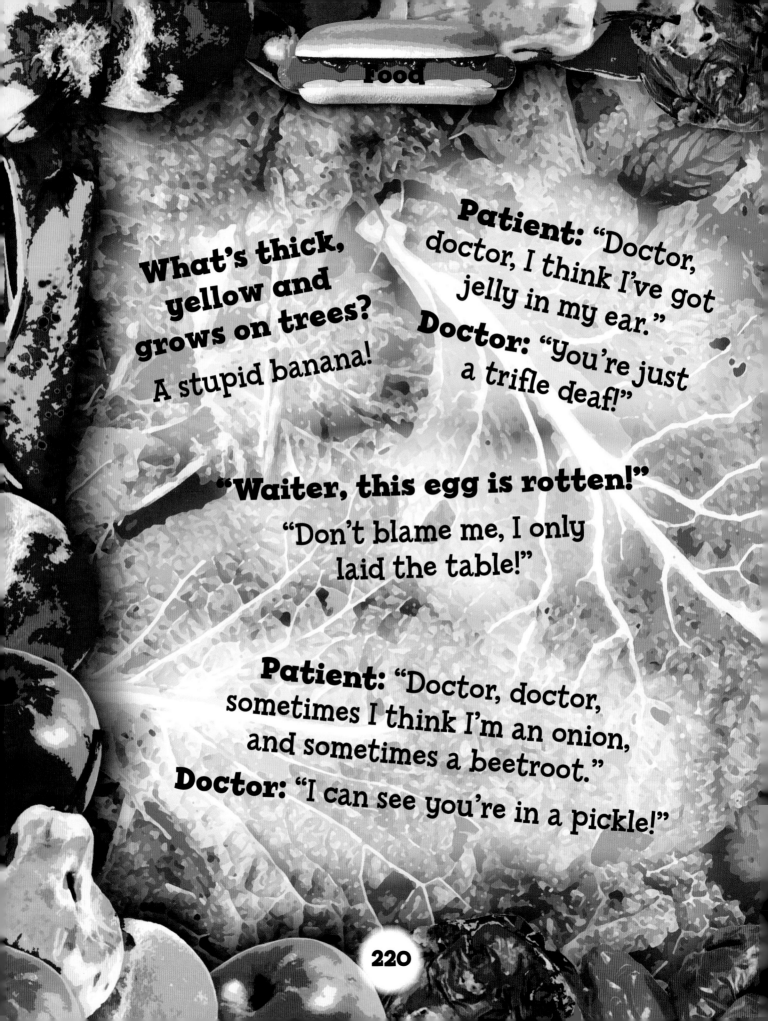

What's thick, yellow and grows on trees?

A stupid banana!

Patient: "Doctor, doctor, I think I've got jelly in my ear."

Doctor: "You're just a trifle deaf!"

"Waiter, this egg is rotten!"

"Don't blame me, I only laid the table!"

Patient: "Doctor, doctor, sometimes I think I'm an onion, and sometimes a beetroot."

Doctor: "I can see you're in a pickle!"

What is a shark's dessert of choice?

Jellyfish!

"Waiter, there's a fly on my steak."

"That's because they seem to be attracted to rotting meat!"

"Waiter, there's a spider in my soup."

"It must have eaten the fly!"

How do you make a banana shake?

Sneak up on it and scream!

Did you hear about the carrot that died?

There was a big turn-up at the funeral!

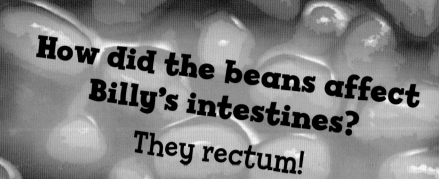

How did the beans affect Billy's intestines?

They rectum!

"Waiter, there's a fly in my soup."

"No sir, that's a cockroach, the fly is on your role!"

"Waiter, this soup tastes funny!"

"Then why aren't you laughing?"

Patient: "Doctor, doctor, what's wrong with me?"

Doctor: "Well, you have sweetcorn up your nose and a sausage in your ear. I'd say you're not eating right!"

What's a ghost's choice of meal?

Goulash!

"Waiter, there's a cockroach in my soup."

"Sorry, Sir, all out of flies!"

What do skeletons say to each other before eating a meal?

"Bone-appetite!"

What did one teddy bear say to the other teddy bear when they were offered dessert?

"No thanks, I'm stuffed!"

How did the jury find the hamburger?

Grill-ty as charred!

How do gossipy burgers spend their time?

They chew the fat!

"Waiter, there's a fly in my soup."

"Don't worry, they don't drink much!"

What did the mayonnaise say when the fridge door opened?

"Close the door, I'm dressing!"

What's worse than finding a slug in your apple?

Finding half a slug in your apple!

What do you call a girl with sausages on her head?

Barbie!

"Waiter, what's this fly doing on my ice cream?"

"It looks like he's learning to ski!"

What nuts are always covered in bogies?

Cashews!

What's the scariest fruit?

A Boo-nana!

What's a ghost's preferred jelly?

Lemon and Slime!

What's the rudest vegetable?

A pea!

"Waiter, there's a huge bug in my soup!"

"Be quiet, Sir, everyone will want one!"

What does a termite eat for breakfast?

Oak-meal!

"Waiter, how did this fly get in my soup?"

"It flew!"

What do devils drink?

Demon-ade!

What's a vampire's preferred fruit?

Blood Orange!

How do you make a swiss roll?

Push him down a hill!

Mum: "Haven't you finished filling the salt shaker yet?"

Matt: "Not yet, it's really hard to get the salt through all those little holes!"

What's yellow and stupid?

Thick custard!

What do monsters call knights in armor?

Tinned food!

Why did the man drown in his muesli?

He was pulled under by a strong currant!

What does a cannibal call the phone book?

The takeaway menu!

"Waiter, why is your thumb on my steak?"

"I don't want to drop it again!"

What's the most musical part of a turkey?

The drumstick!

Did you hear about the man who put his false teeth in backwards?

He ate himself!

A family of three tomatoes were walking in town one day when the baby tomato started to fall behind. Big daddy tomato walked back to baby tomato, stomped on her and said, "Ketchup!"

How do monsters like their eggs on a morning?

Terri-fried!

Why do idiots eat biscuits?

Because they're crackers!

What do zombies eat for breakfast?

Dreaded wheat!

Why did the monster trample all over his cornflakes?

He was a cereal killer!

"Waiter, do you have frogs' legs?"

"How dare you! I've always walked like this!"

Did you hear about the cannibal who was late for lunch?

He was given the cold shoulder!

What did the grape do when the elephant sat on it?

Let out a little wine!

Which martial artist lives in a pod?

Bruce Pea!

What do witches like to eat as a summer time treat?

Leeches and cream!

What do you get if you cross a biscuit with a monster?

Crumbs!

Why do pixies eat their food so quickly?

Because they're always goblin!

What do you get if you cross a monster with peanut butter?

A monster that sticks to the roof of your mouth!

How do you make a monster float?

Take two scoops of ice-cream, a glass of cola and add one monster!

What does Dracula have for breakfast?

Ready-neck!

What's purple and hums?

A rotten plum!

Did you hear about the monster who went on a crash diet?

He wrecked three cars and a bus!

What do monsters eat for dessert?

Boo-berry pie!

"Waiter, there's a small insect in my soup."

"My apologies sir, I shall fetch you a larger one!"

What is yellow and white and throws itself off the edge of the table?

A lemming meringue!

What's the difference between an interfering neighbor and a naked apple?

One is rude and nosy. The other is nude and rosy!

On which day do monsters eat people?

Chews-day!

What do hedgehogs enjoy as an afternoon snack?

Prickled onions!

What do you get from naughty cows?

Bad milk!

What's the difference between Frankenstein's monster and boiled potatoes?

You can't mash Frankenstein's monster!

How do you save lamb chops from drowning?

Put them in gravy boats!

Where can you learn to make ice-cream?

At sundae school!

Why should you stay calm when meeting a cannibal?

Otherwise you would be in a stew!

"Waiter, is there any soup on the menu?"

"No sir, I wiped it all off!"

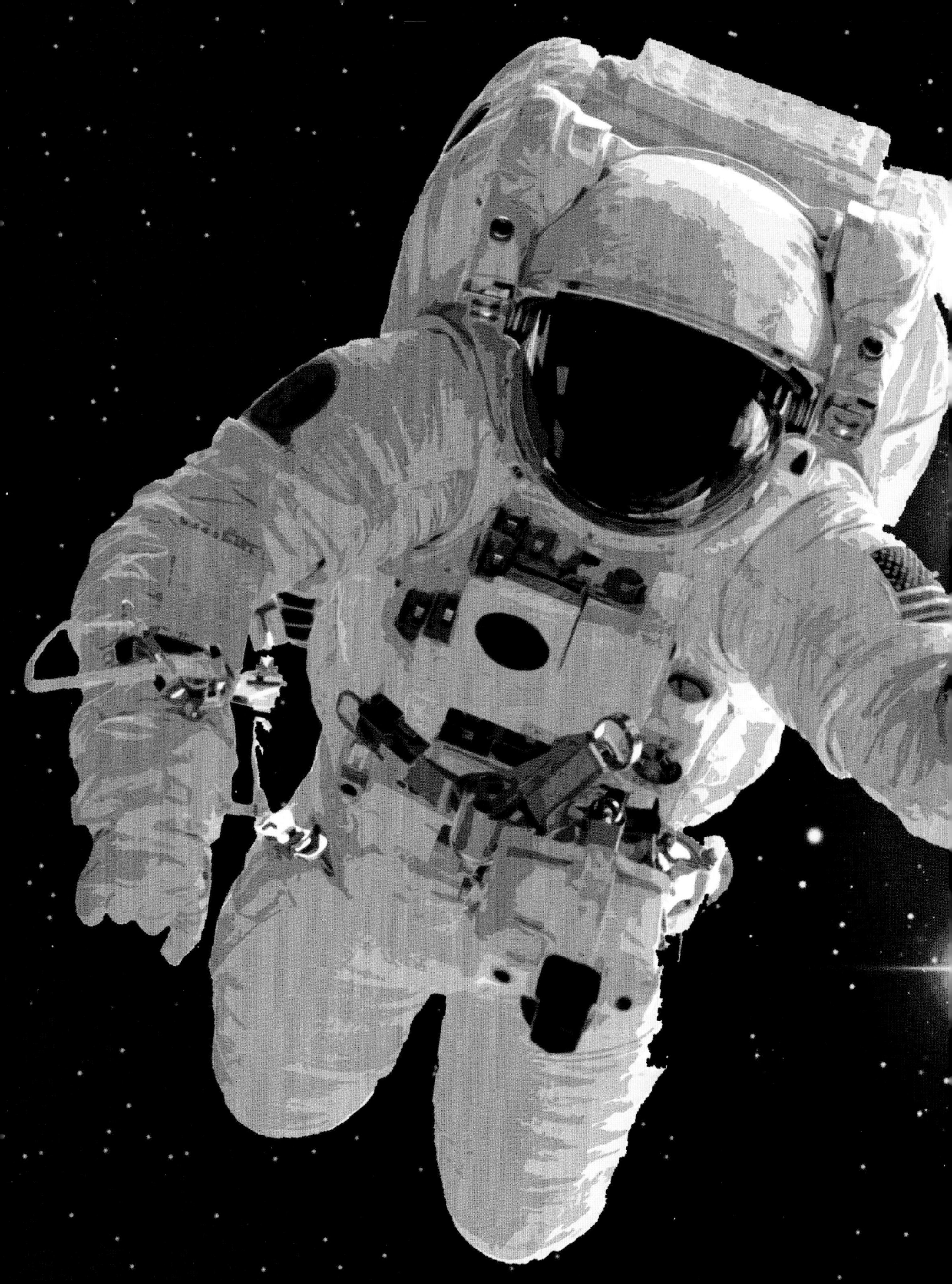

Space

Patient: "Doctor, doctor, I keep seeing green aliens with five eyes and three legs."

Doctor: "Have you seen a psychiatrist?"

Patient: "No just green aliens with five eyes and three legs!"

What's an alien's choice of snack?

A Milky Way!

What did one alien plant say to the other?

"Take me to your weeder!"

What did E.T.'s mum say when he returned home?

"Where on earth have you been?"

Where do astronauts leave their spaceships?

At parking meteors!

What do you call a crazy spaceman?

An astro-nut!

How do you get a baby alien to sleep?

Rocket!

What do you call a wizard from space?

A flying sorcerer!

Why did the cow go into space?

He wanted to see the mooooon!

How did Darth Vader know what Luke Skywalker was getting for Christmas?

He felt his presents!

What do aliens play with their friends?

Moon-opoly!

How do you address an angry looking alien with a ray gun?

Very politely!

If Martians live on Mars and Venusians live on Venus, who lives on Pluto?

Fleas!

Did you hear about the man who was captured by extra-terrestrial teddy bears?

He had a close encounter of the furred kind!

Why was the alien dog so itchy?

He had luna-tics!

What's green and goes 'Beep, beep'?

An alien in a traffic jam!

Can you destroy a Dalek by throwing eggs at him?

Of course, he'd be eggs-terminated!

How does an alien count to 23?

On its fingers!

What alien has the best hearing?

The eeriest!

What did the martian say to the gas pump?

"Take your fingers out of your ears when I'm talking to you!"

What do you call an overweight alien?

An extra-cholesterol!

What do you call an alien with no eyes?

Alan!

Which sweets do aliens like best?

Martian-mallows!

Why should you never insult an alien?

You might hurt its feelers!

Why do aliens keep flying past Peter Pan's house?

Because it says 'Never Never Land'!

How did the rocket lose its job?

It got fired!

What cartoons do Martians watch?

Lunar Tunes!

Knock, knock.

Who's there?

Olive.

Olive who?

Olive in a flying saucer.

If an athlete gets athlete's foot, what does an astronaut get?

Missile-toe!

Why did the aliens get thrown out of the hotel?

They were flying the saucers!

Why are aliens green?

Because they forgot to take their travel-sickness tablets!

What sort of star is dangerous?

A shooting star.

What is E.T. short for?

He has little legs!

What's Dracula's preferred sci-fi movie?

The Vampire Strikes Back!

What has eight legs and flies through space?

An unidentified flying octopus!

What's green on the inside, but grey on the outside and has a big trunk?

An alien disguised as an elephant!

What do aliens wear to weddings?

Space suits!

What sci-fi film is about an angry referee?

The Umpire Strikes Back!

Mum alien: "Don't eat that uranium."
Little alien: "Why not?"
Mum alien: "You'll get atomic-ache!"

What do you call an alien spaceship with broken air-conditioning?

A frying saucer!

What's green, wrinkly and has no teeth?

An alien grandad!

What's green and hairy?

An alien with a beard!

Why did Captain Kirk go into the ladies toilet?

To boldly go where no man has been before!

Why is lightning so badly behaved?

It doesn't know how to conduct itself!

What part of the keyboard do aliens like best?

The space bar!

Knock, knock.

Who's there?

Ann.

Ann who?

Ann Droid!

Did you hear about the alien with five legs?

His jeans fit him like a glove!

What sea is in space?

The galax-sea!

How do you know when the moon isn't hungry?

When it's full!

How can you tell when a robot is mad?

He goes screwy!

What did the robot eat for a light snack?

A 100-watt light bulb!

Why don't astronauts get hungry after being blasted into space?

Because they've just had a big launch!

What does an astronaut do when he gets angry?

He blasts off!

What is green, has two heads, three arms, five feet and six eyes?

An alien with spare parts!

What kind of saddle do you put on a space horse?

A saddle-lite!

Why is Saturn called Saturn?

Because it has a nice ring to it!

Where do aliens drink beer?

At a mars bar!

How does the solar system keep its trousers up?

With an asteroid belt!

Knock, knock.

Who's there?

Armageddon.

Armageddon who?

Armageddon out of here, the aliens have landed!

What do you call an alien star ship that drips water and bogeys?

A crying saucer!

Why couldn't the astronaut book a room on the moon?

Because it was full!

What should you do if you come across a blue alien?

Tell him a joke!

What did the alien win in a raffle?

The constellation prize!

How did the astronaut serve drinks?

In sun-glasses!

What do you call a Jedi teacher who sits on the floor cross legged?

Yoga!

Why are aliens great gardeners?

They have green fingers!

How does an alien shave?

With a laser blade!

Doctor Who has a new range of herbs and spices out.

Well, he is a thyme lord!

What do you get if you cross a Jedi teacher with a bear?

Yoda Bear!

What do you call a planet full of nasty aliens?

A waste of space!

How do you get 33 little aliens into your fridge?

Open the door!

Why do spacemen wear bullet proof vests?

Because of all the shooting stars!

Space

Knock, knock.
Who's There?
Art.
Art Who?
R2-D2!

Why did the spaceman go to the optician?
He had stars in his eyes!

Why was the space robot so silly?
It had a screw loose!

What happened when Anakin threw moon dust at Jar Jar Binks?
Jar Jar Blinked!

Why wouldn't you want Saturn to have a bath at your house?

He'd leave a filthy ring around the tub!

What do space monsters eat for a light snack?

Space-chips!

What do you get if you cross a Martian with a golf score?

A little green bogey!

If a meteor hits earth we call it a meteorite. What do we call the ones that miss?

Meteor-ongs!